Hotel Bristol

Elisabeth Hölzl **Hotel Bristol**

Folio Verlag Wien/Bozen

Editor
Antonella Cattani Contemporary Art, Bolzano | www.accart.com
ArtMbassy Berlin/Rome | www.artmbassy.com
Folio Verlag Wien/Bozen

Grafic Design
Elisabeth Hölzl

Translations
Claudia Sacchetto, Leila Kais

Printing
Longo AG Bozen

© Elisabeth Hölzl and authors
© Folio Verlag Wien/Bozen 2008
All rights reserved

ISBN 978-3-85256-407-4
ISBN 978-88-6299-000-4 (Italy)

www.folioverlag.com

9 – 11 Ausgecheckt – ein fotografischer Abriss | Matthias Dusini

13 – 27 **Halls**

29 – 31 Fuori uso – un abbozzo fotografico | Matthias Dusini

33 – 45 **Rooms**

47 – 49 Checked Out – A Photographic Sketch Book | Matthias Dusini

51 – 111 **Pool, chairs, colors**

113 – 131 Hotel Bristol. Die Geschichte | La storia | The Story | Josef Rohrer

Ausgecheckt – ein fotografischer Abriss
Matthias Dusini

Über zwei Jahre lang besuchte Elisabeth Hölzl das leer stehende Hotel Bristol in der Meraner Otto-Huber-Straße. Dabei entstand weniger eine nüchterne Dokumentation des Gebäudes als das Tagebuch einer Beziehung, die die Künstlerin zu einem rätselhaften Ort im Zentrum ihrer Stadt aufbaute. Die Kamera streift aus geringer Entfernung über die Oberflächen der Räume und bleibt an Details hängen – Stuhllehnen, Spiegel, samtenen Vorhängen und weißen Schutzbezügen. Diese Nahsicht verleiht den Bildern eine sinnliche Natürlichkeit, als könnte man mit dem Finger über den Staub fahren, der sich auf den Möbeln gesammelt hat. Klassische Architekturfotografie hat die Funktion, ein Gebäude vor seinem Gebrauch abzubilden. Elisabeth Hölzl zeigt ein aufgebrauchtes Gebäude, und zwar so, als wollte sie es am Leben erhalten. Es sind gewissermaßen Werbefotos für eine Ruine. Leer stehende Hotels wurden durch Stanley Kubricks Film „Shining" zum Topos des Unheimlichen, zum Tummelplatz abgründiger Imagination. Der amerikanische Architekturtheoretiker Anthony Vidler legte in seinem Buch „The Architectural Uncanny" (1992) das Unheimliche als konstituierenden Parameter moderner Raumauffassung dar. Elisabeth Hölzls Fotos polen die einschlägig besetzte Aura solcher vermeintlich fremder Räume um. Sonnenstrahlen dringen in die Räume, ein Meer weißer Möbelüberzüge in einem lichtdurchfluteten Saal erinnert an einen fröhlichen Gespensteraufstand. Leblos wirken daneben die alten Werbepostkarten von Bar und Speisesaal des ehemaligen Hotels. Kommerzielle Bilder filtern Flecken aus Gesichtern und Risse aus Gebäuden, während diese Fotos ihre mimetische Sinnlichkeit gerade über solche Fehler entfalten.

In ihrer Fotoarbeit für das von E. Tauber herausgegebene Buch „Sinti und Roma – eine Spurensuche" besuchte Elisabeth Hölzl über einen längeren Zeitraum hinweg die Romasiedlung in Bozen. Dieser alltägliche Umgang mit den abgebildeten Personen verändert auch die Qualität des fotografischen Apparats. Er ist keine neutrale Maschine mehr, die Objekte festhält, sondern der Zeuge einer Beziehung, die sich zwischen der Fotografin und der Romafamilie entwickelt. Damit greift Elisabeth Hölzl die Kritik am ethnografischen Blick auf, die darin besteht, dass die Fähigkeit der Ethnografie in Abrede gestellt wurde, mit vermeintlicher wissenschaftlicher Neutralität Symbolsysteme fremder Kulturen aufzuzeichnen. Auch ihre Annäherung an das Hotel Bristol folgt dieser Logik eines selbstreflexiven ethnografischen Blicks. Ein verlassenes Hotel ohne offensichtliche architektonische Qualität ließe sich auch als Synonym eines wertlosen Objekts betrachten, das der ungestraften Zerstörung ausgeliefert ist. Elisabeth Hölzl lädt diese dem Vergessen preisgegebenen Räume symbolisch auf, ihre Patina als besondere atmosphärische Qualität unterstreichend. Der deutsche Philosoph Gernot Böhme definiert Atmosphäre als Prototyp eines „Zwischenphänomens", als etwas, das zwischen Subjekt und Objekt liegt. Elisabeth Hölzls Fotografien konzentrieren sich auf die atmosphärischen Werte dieser Räume, deren Formen zugunsten ihrer Ausstrahlung in den Hintergrund treten.

Elisabeth Hölzl legte erst einen Fundus von Fotografien an, dann folgten Überlegungen, nach welchen Kriterien dieses Material geordnet und schließlich gezeigt werden soll. Sowohl durch das Format der ausgesuchten Fotos als auch durch deren Reihenfolge interpretiert die Künstlerin das Archiv, das darüber definiert ist, dass es lediglich ein Ordnungssystem, aber keine semantische Klassifikation zur Verfügung stellt. In diese bis zum Layout des Buches reichenden formalen Entscheidungen der Künstlerin fließt jenes Wissen ein, das sie bei dem Verweilen an dem fotografierten Ort erwarb. Aus einer Architekturdokumentation wird die Interpretation eines Gebäudes. Die mimetische Wirkung des vergrößerten Einzelbildes steht im Kontrast zu den Bildserien, die eine strukturelle Aussage vermitteln. So reiht sie im Buch Fotos von Stühlen aneinander, sodass der Eindruck monotoner Serialität entsteht. Stockwerk um Stockwerk wiederholt sich derselbe Grundriss und dieselbe Abfolge grün, rot, gelb und lila gestrichener Räume, sodass Zimmer Nummer 210 genau unter Zimmer 310 liegt und ident ist mit Zimmer 410. Exklusivität, nicht serielle Austauschbarkeit, ist das Dienstleistungsversprechen von Hotelbetrieben. Daher muss die standardisierte Zellenstruktur des Gebäudes den Augen des Gastes verborgen bleiben; sie wird erst in Elisabeth Hölzls Dokumentation sichtbar.

Die Reihung der Fotografien hat auch die Funktion, die voranschreitende Demolierung des Hotels, seine allmähliche Entkleidung chronologisch darzustellen. Allmählich schält sich der Rohbau heraus, entblößt sich die Tektonik unter jener durch Werbung und Zeitungsberichten ästhetisch überhöhten Luxustextur der Anfangsjahre. Immer mehr Gegenstände verschwinden aus den Zimmern, ein Glas hinterlässt auf einer Tischplatte einen Rand, ein heller Fleck an der Wand markiert, wo einmal ein Spiegel hing. Am Ende werden als einzige Spuren des Gebäudes Fotografien bleiben. Die Kamera friert einen Prozess voranschreitender Dematerialisierung ein, der, bevor er abgeschlossen ist, der Architektur neue Bedeutungen verleiht. Besonders deutlich wird dies am eigentlichen Herzstück des Hotels, der großzügigen Poollandschaft am Dach. Das leere Becken und die halbverfallenen Aufbauten mit schlanken Säulen geben dem Ort eine kultisch anmutende Bedeutung, als würde hier eine archäologische Grabung stattfinden, in der ein Heiligtum oder ein Tempel freigelegt wird.

Im Frühjahr 2006 affichierte die Künstlerin in den Straßen Merans Plakate mit Fotos aus dem Inneren des Hotel Bristol. Sie lenkte damit die Aufmerksamkeit auf ein Gebäude, das den Einheimischen stets ein Fremdkörper geblieben war. Kurz vor dem Abriss des Hotels lösten die Plakate ein lautes „Warum?" aus. Die architektonische Postmoderne des letzten Drittel des 20. Jahrhunderts definierte sich im deutschsprachigen Raum gerade auch über die Erhaltung historischer Stadtkerne. Aldo Rossi kritisierte in seinem Buch *L'architettura della città* 1966 die Totalplanung des modernen Städtebaus und unterstrich den identitätsbildenden Wert historischer Monumente. Auch der Architektur der Hochmoderne wird inzwischen ein Denkmalwert zugesprochen. Was aber passiert mit Gebäuden, die aus dem Katalog des kulturellen Erbes herausfallen? Die Architektur der Nachkriegszeit hat diesbezüglich einen schweren Stand. Das ungeliebte Bristol ist inzwischen verschwunden wie ein ungebetener, allzu lang gebliebener Gast. Auch dem Gebäude der vor wenigen Jahren demolierten Thermenanlage S.A.L.V.A.R., ein ungleich anspruchsvolleres Projekt des Architekten Willi Gutweniger von 1972, das von Elisabeth Hölzl ebenfalls dokumentiert wurde, weint niemand eine Träne nach.

In einer touristischen Gegend wird die Architektur besonders stark von den Innovationszyklen kommerzieller Verwertung verschlissen, seit jeher: Das Bristol wie auch die Thermen wurden am Standort ehemaliger Grand Hotels errichtet. Was die funktionalistische Programmatik der Moderne unterschlug, dass die piktoriale Bedeutung die tektonisch-strukturelle überstrahlt, wird hier evident. Gebäude sollen starke Bilder sein, die durch neue ersetzt werden, sobald sie ihren Signalcharakter verloren haben; Las Vegas ist das bekannteste Beispiel dafür. Ähnlich wie bei alten Ozeandampfern wird nicht an eine Sanierung oder Umrüstung gedacht. *Usa e getta*: Nach ihrem Gebrauch werden Schiffe zu Altmetall verarbeitet, Hotels ausgeweidet und abgerissen. Elisabeth Hölzl setzt dieser konsumistischen Zeitlogik eine der kontemplativen Raumbesetzung entgegen. Sie ruft damit allerdings nicht zu einer Rettung des Gebäudes auf, sondern beschränkt sich auf die Geste des Zeigens. Sie nähert sich dem Hotel wie einem gestrandeten Wal, dessen baldigen Tod sie nicht verhehlen kann. Ihre emphatischen Fotos weisen darauf hin, dass eine Stadt, die Architektur nur als tote Baumasse betrachtet, auch ihre Identität verliert.

Fuori uso – un abbozzo fotografico   Matthias Dusini

Elisabeth Hölzl per più di due anni ha fotografato gli ambienti deserti dell'Hotel Bristol in via Otto Huber a Merano. Da questa esperienza, più che una documentazione oggettiva dell'edificio, è nato il diario del rapporto tra l'artista e un luogo misterioso nel centro della sua città. Il suo obiettivo sfiora le superfici soffermandosi sui dettagli: schienali di sedie, specchi, tende di velluto, teli bianchi. Questo sguardo ravvicinato conferisce alle immagini una naturalezza sensuale, dando la sensazione di poter passare il dito sulla polvere che si è depositata sui mobili. La classica fotografia d'architettura ha la funzione di ritrarre un edificio prima del suo utilizzo. Elisabeth Hölzl ne mostra uno in disuso e lo fa come se volesse tenerlo in vita. In un certo senso sono foto pubblicitarie per una rovina. Dopo *Shining* di Stanley Kubrick gli alberghi disabitati sono diventati un *topos* dell'inquietante, un luogo del mistero e dell'immaginazione. E l'inquietante, secondo il teorico dell'architettura americano Anthony Vidler (*The Architectural Uncanny, 1992*), è un parametro costitutivo della concezione moderna dello spazio. Le fotografie di Elisabeth Hölzl, invece, capovolgono la percezione di questi ambienti che potrebbero risultare estranei. Dei raggi di sole penetrano nelle stanze, un mare di teli bianchi posati sui mobili in una sala inondata di luce ricorda un'allegra brigata di fantasmi. In confronto, le vecchie cartoline pubblicitarie che riproducono il bar e la sala da pranzo dell'ex hotel sembrano senza vita. Nelle foto commerciali le macchie sui volti e le crepe sui muri vengono ritoccate, mentre la sensualità mimetica di queste immagini scaturisce proprio da tali imperfezioni.

Per realizzare il lavoro fotografico raccolto nel libro curato da Elisabeth Tauber *Sinti und Roma – eine Spurensuche* ("Sinti e Rom: sulle tracce di un popolo") Elisabeth Hölzl ha frequentato per un lungo periodo il campo rom di Bolzano. Il rapporto quotidiano con le persone ritratte cambia anche il carattere della macchina fotografica. Essa non è più una macchina neutrale che immortala gli oggetti, bensì il testimone di un rapporto che si sviluppa tra la fotografa e le famiglie rom. In questo modo Elisabeth Hölzl riprende la critca all'etnografia che mette in dubbio la capacità di questa disciplina di descrivere culture straniere con imparzialità scientifica. Il suo accostarsi all'Hotel Bristol può essere paragonato ad uno sguardo etnografico "autocritico", consapevole cioè del proprio coinvolgimento con l'oggetto indagato. Un albergo abbandonato privo di evidenti pregi architettonici potrebbe anche essere sinonimo di un oggetto senza valore in balia della distruzione. Elisabeth Hölzl carica di simboli questi ambienti destinati ad essere dimenticati, mettendo in evidenza l'atmosfera particolare che vi regna. Il filosofo tedesco Gernot Böhme definisce quest'ultima prototipo di un "fenomeno intermedio", qualcosa che sta tra soggetto e oggetto. Le fotografie di Elisabeth Hölzl si concentrano sui significati dell'atmosfera in questi ambienti, la cui forma passa in secondo piano rispetto alla loro espressività.

Elisabeth Hölzl prima ha raccolto una serie di fotografie, poi ha riflettuto sui criteri in base ai quali ordinare e presentare questo materiale. Sia attraverso il formato sia attraverso la sequenza delle foto scelte l'artista interpreta il suo archivio, che fornisce soltanto una classificazione sistematica ma non semantica. In queste decisioni formali dell'artista, che riguardano anche il layout del libro, confluiscono le conoscenze da lei acquisite nei luoghi fotografati. La documentazione architettonica diventa l'interpretazione dell'edificio. L'effetto mimetico della singola immagine ingrandita è in contrasto con le serie fotografiche che trasmettono un messaggio strutturale. Così nel libro vengono poste una accanto all'altra immagini di sedie nella loro monotona serialità. Ad ogni piano si ripete la stessa successione di camere dipinte di verde, rosso, giallo e lilla, cosicché la stanza numero 210 si trova esattamente sotto la stanza 310 ed è identica alla stanza 410. Gli hotel garantiscono tra i loro servizi l'esclusività, non l'intercambiabilità. Perciò la struttura ad alveare e la standardizzazione dell'edificio rimangono nascoste agli occhi degli ospiti; esse diventano visibili soltanto nella documentazione di Elisabeth Hölzl.

La disposizione delle fotografie ha anche la funzione di rappresentare cronologicamente la progressiva demolizione dell'hotel, il suo graduale svuotamento. A poco a poco si rivela la costruzione grezza, si scopre la struttura dietro la facciata di un edificio di lusso la cui estetica è stata esaltata nei primi anni di attività dalla pubblicità e dai giornali. Sempre più oggetti scompaiono dalle stanze, un bicchiere lascia un alone sul piano di un tavolo, una macchia chiara sulla parete indica il punto in cui una volta era appeso uno specchio. Alla fine rimarranno, uniche tracce dell'edificio, delle fotografie. La macchina fotografica coglie un processo di progressiva dematerializzazione che, prima di essere concluso, conferisce all'architettura nuovi significati. Ciò risulta particolarmente chiaro nel vero cuore dell'hotel, la grande piscina sul tetto. La vasca vuota e la struttura in rovina scandita da colonne sottili sembrano attribuire all'ambiente un valore di culto, come se fossero in corso degli scavi archeologici per portare alla luce un luogo sacro o un tempio.

Nella primavera del 2006 l'artista ha affisso nelle strade di Merano dei manifesti con le fotografie degli interni dell'Hotel Bristol. In questo modo ha attirato l'attenzione su un edificio che era sempre stato estraneo alla popolazione locale, destando, poco prima della sua demolizione, forti interrogativi. L'architettura postmoderna degli ultimi trent'anni del secolo scorso si distingueva nell'area di lingua tedesca anche per la conservazione dei centri storici. Nel 1966 Aldo Rossi nel suo libro *L'architettura della città* criticava la pianificazione totale dell'urbanistica moderna e sottolineava l'importanza dei monumenti storici per la formazione di un'identità. Nel frattempo anche all'architettura modernista viene riconosciuto un valore storico. Che ne è però degli edifici che non rientrano nell'elenco di quelli che rappresentano un'eredità culturale? L'architettura del dopoguerra è a questo riguardo in una posizione difficile. Lo sgradito Hotel Bristol intanto è scomparso, come un ospite indesiderato rimasto troppo a lungo. A Merano nessuno rimpiange nemmeno l'edificio della S.A.L.V.A.R. che ospitava le Terme e che è stato demolito pochi anni fa – un progetto di gran lunga più ambizioso elaborato dall'architetto Willi Gutweniger e ultimato nel 1972 – anch'esso documentato da Elisabeth Hölzl. In una regione turistica da sempre l'architettura viene fortemente consumata dai cicli innovativi dello sfruttamento commerciale: il Bristol, come le Terme, venne costruito dove una volta sorgeva un Grand Hotel.

Ciò che il funzionalismo dell'epoca moderna teneva nascosto, cioè che il significato pittoriale offusca quello tettonico-strutturale, diventa qui evidente. Gli edifici devono essere immagini forti e vengono sostituiti da nuovi non appena hanno perso il loro significato. Las Vegas ne è l'esempio più noto. Come per i vecchi transatlantici non si pensa a un risanamento o a una riconversione. Usa e getta: dopo il loro utilizzo le navi vengono trasformate in rottame metallico, gli hotel vengono sventrati e demoliti. Elisabeth Hölzl contrappone a questa logica consumistica del tempo una logica contemplativa dello spazio. Non incita comunque a salvare l'edificio, ma si limita a mostrarlo. Si avvicina all'hotel come a una balena arenata, della quale non riesce a nascondere la morte imminente. Le sue empatiche fotografie ricordano che una città, che considera l'architettura soltanto come una massa di edifici senza valore, perde anche la sua identità.

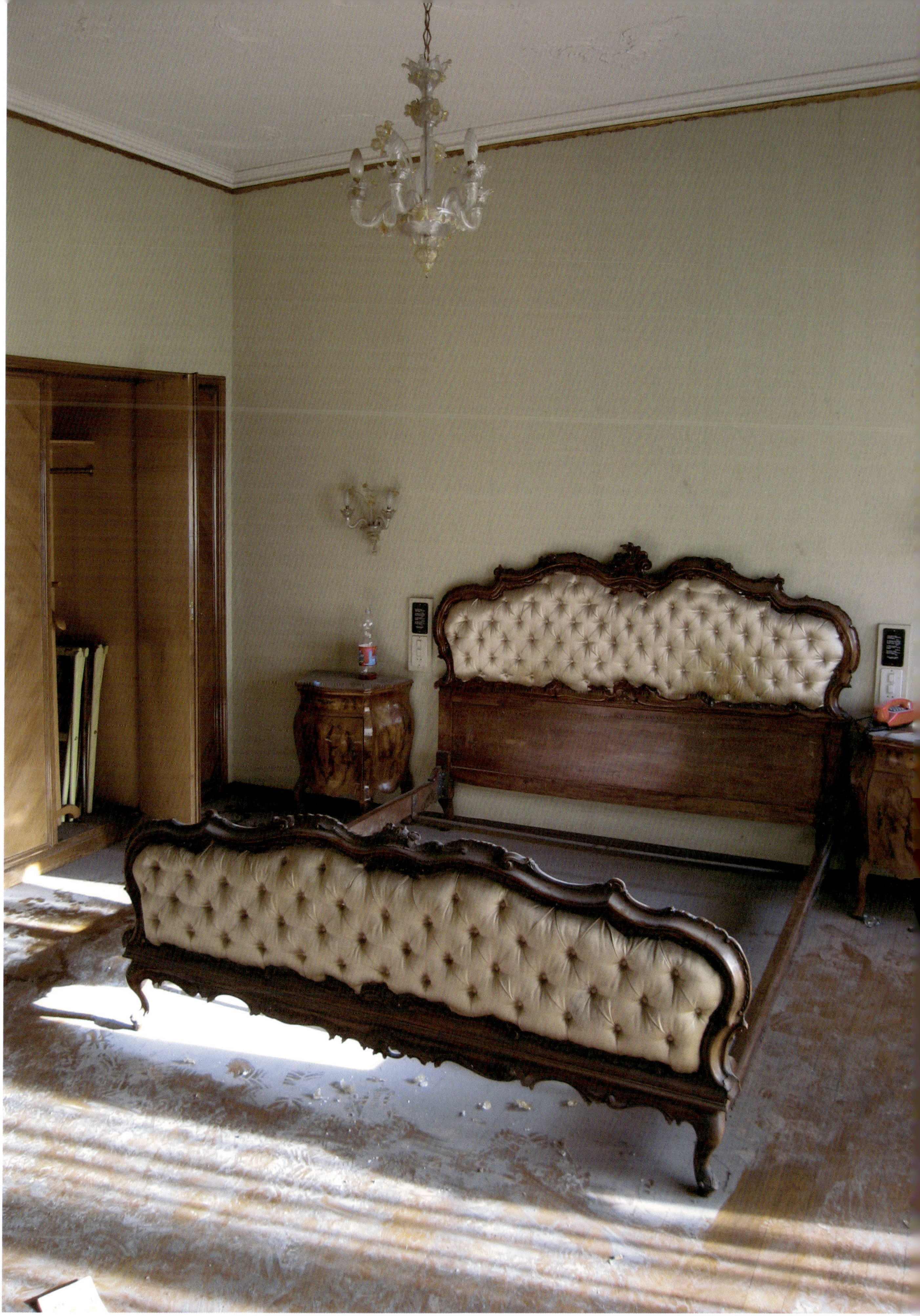

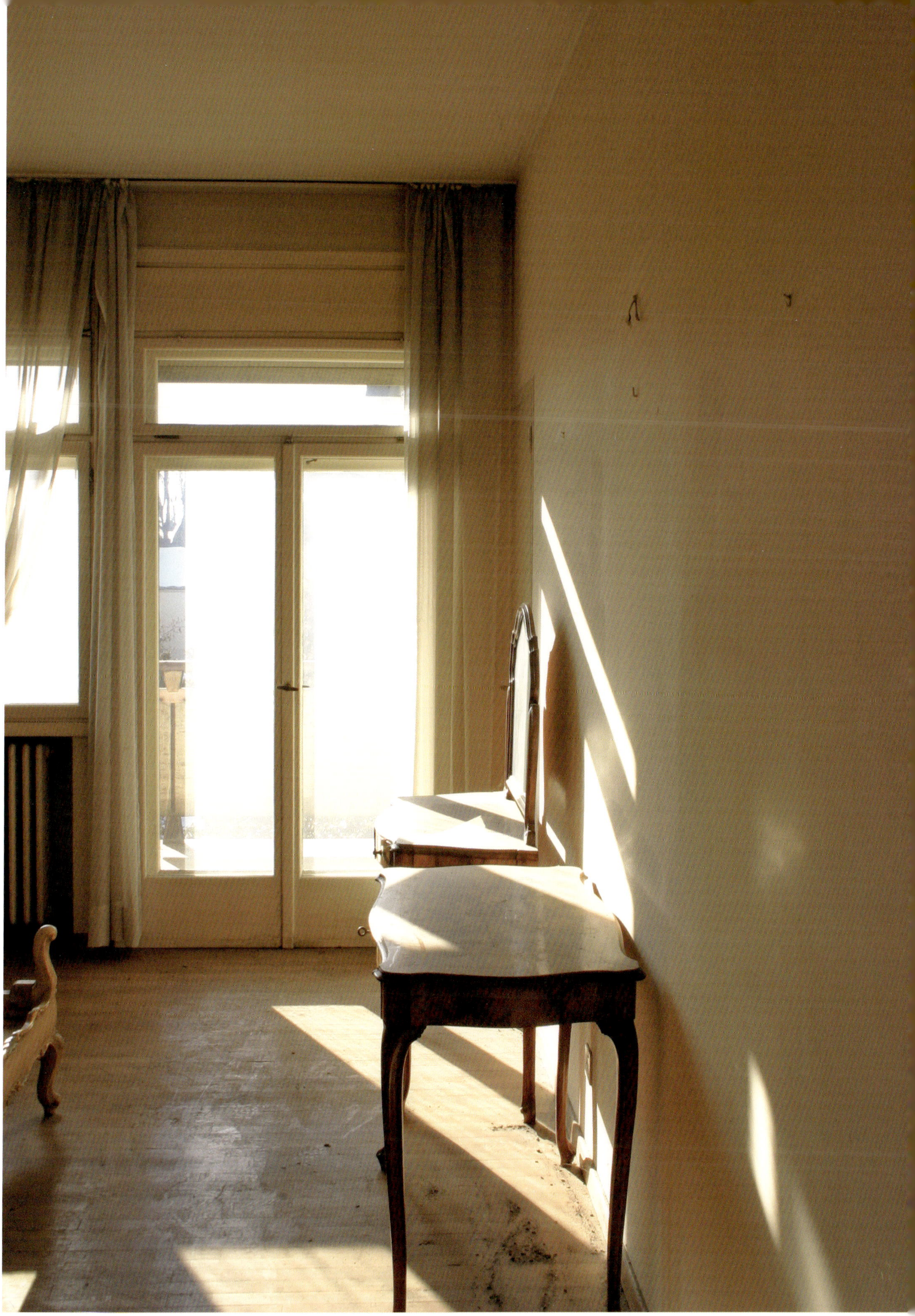

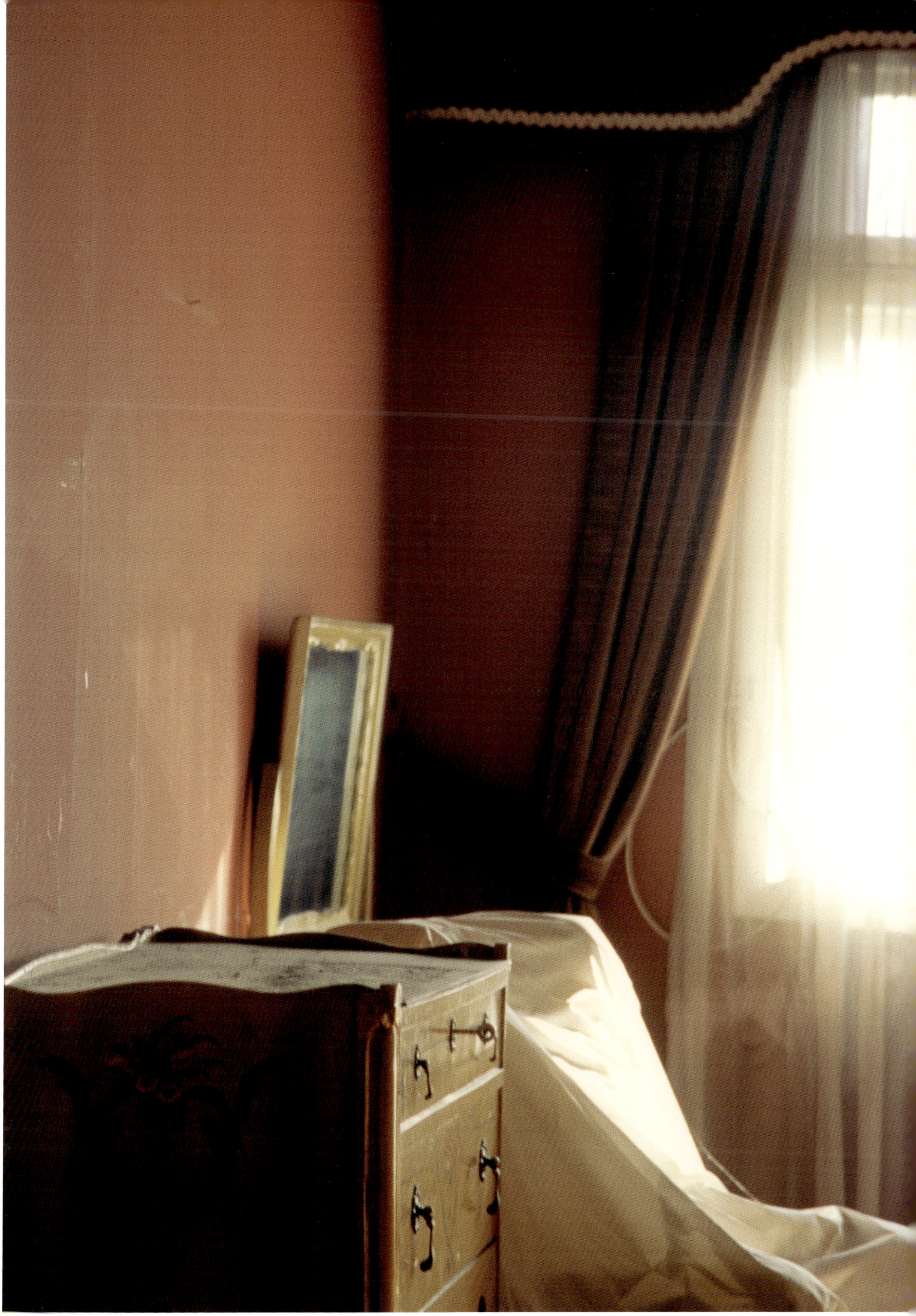

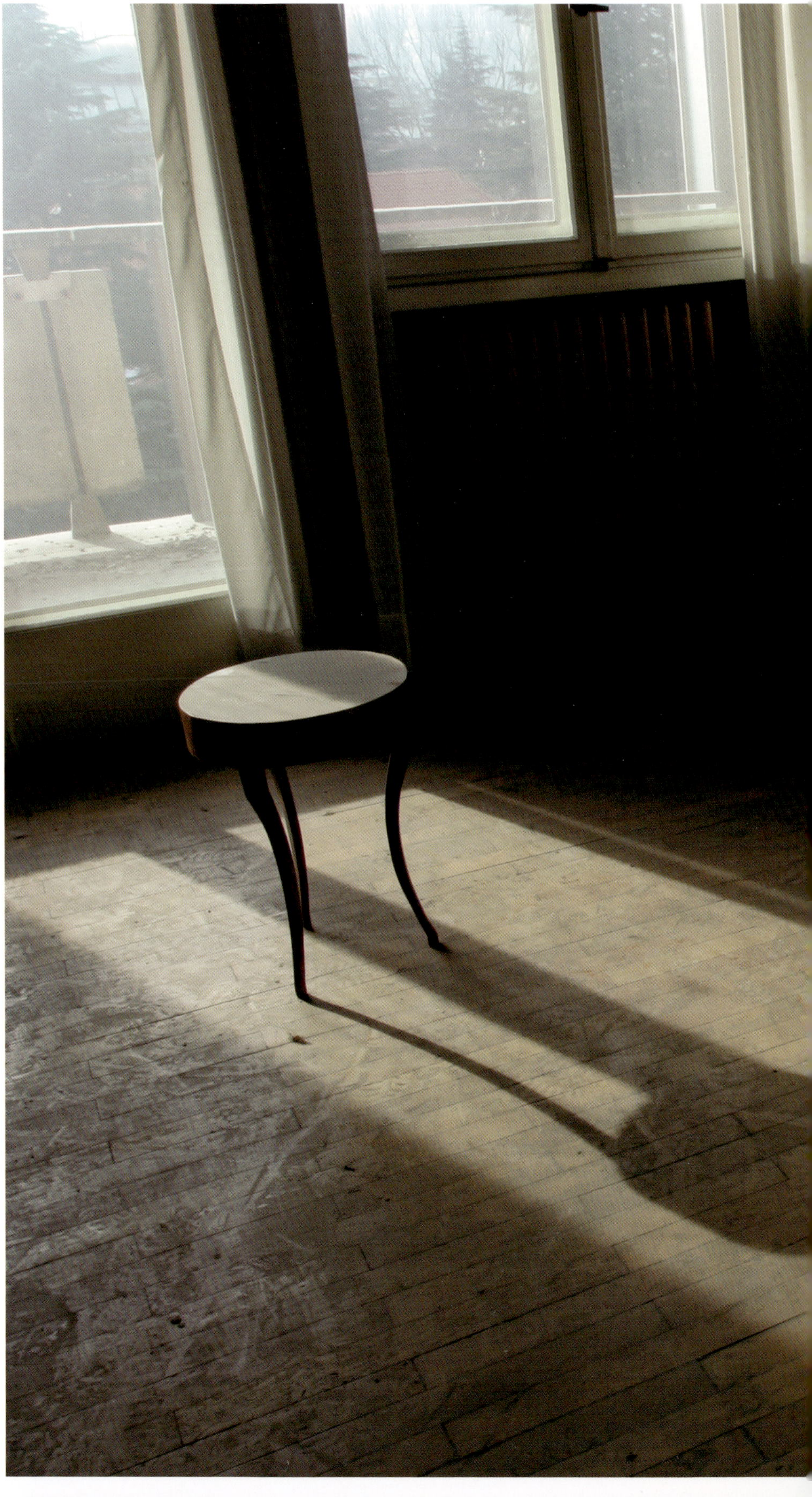

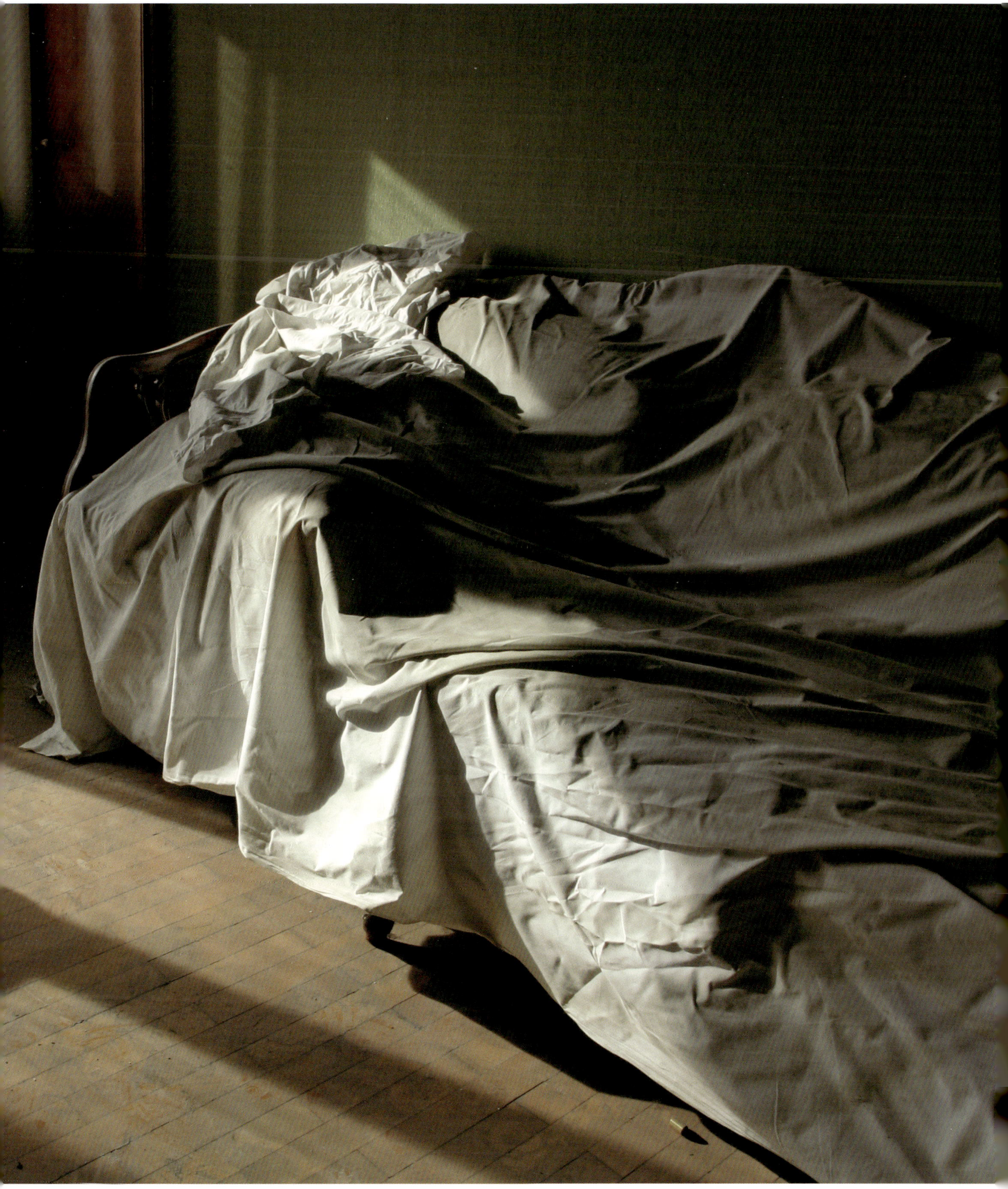

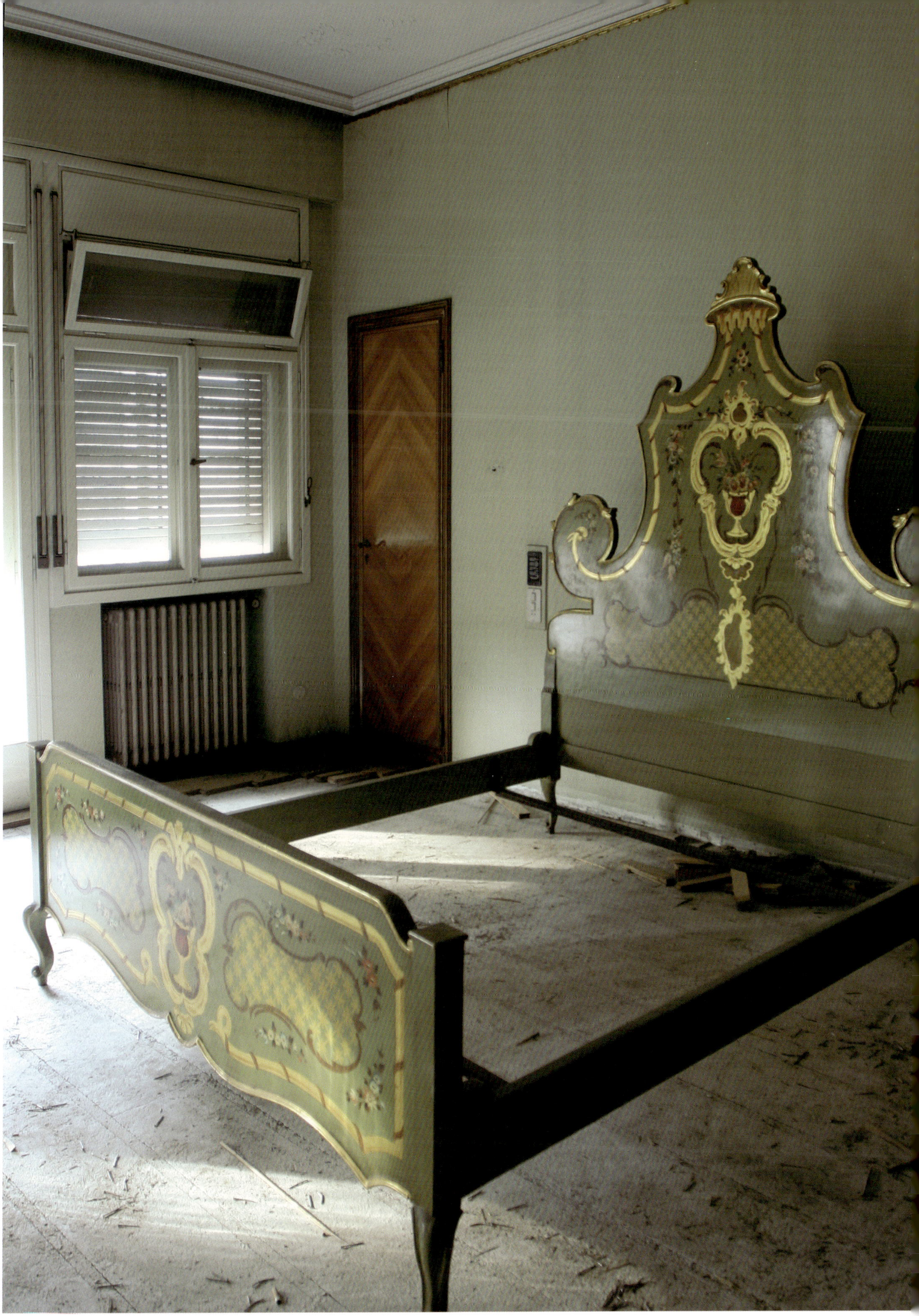

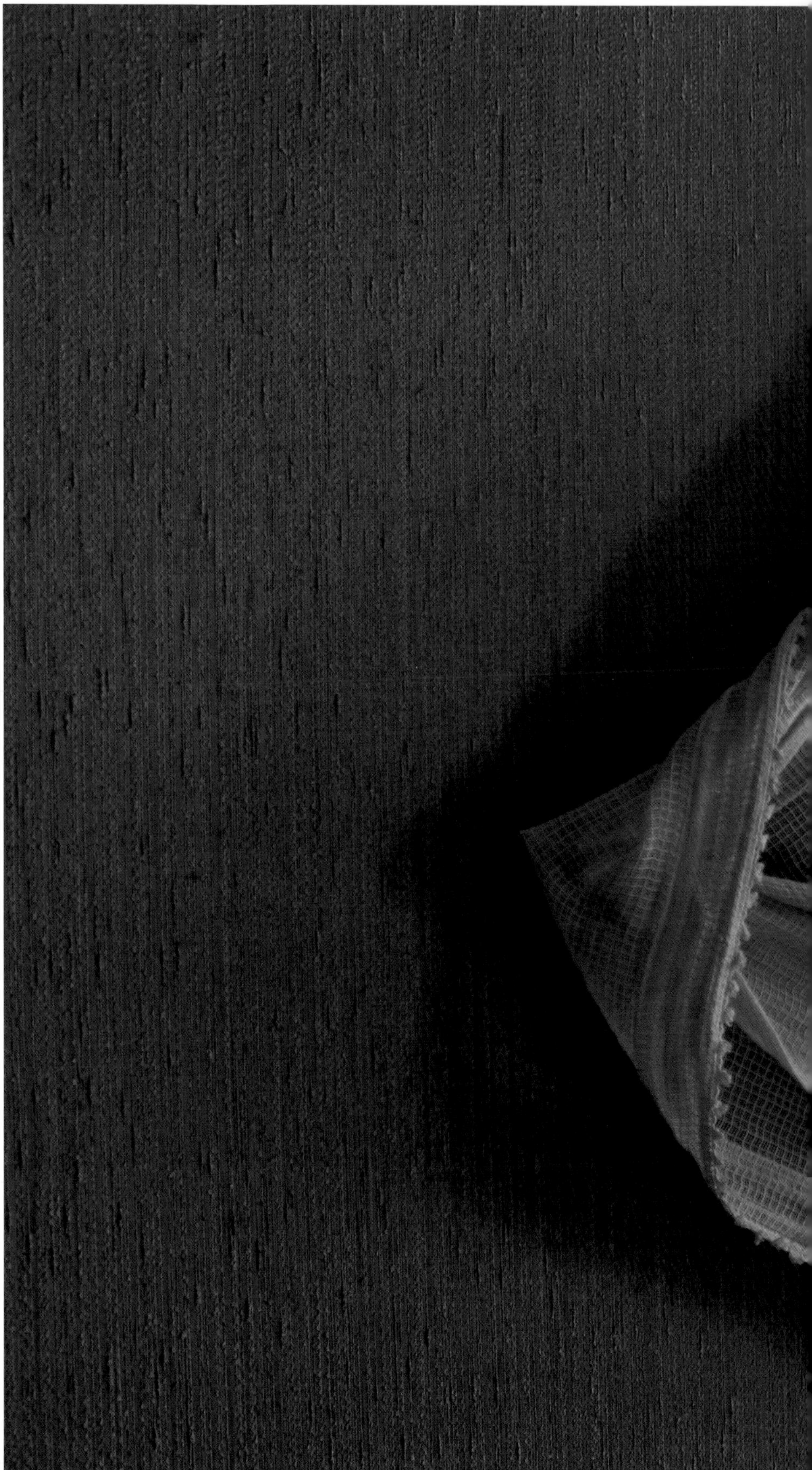

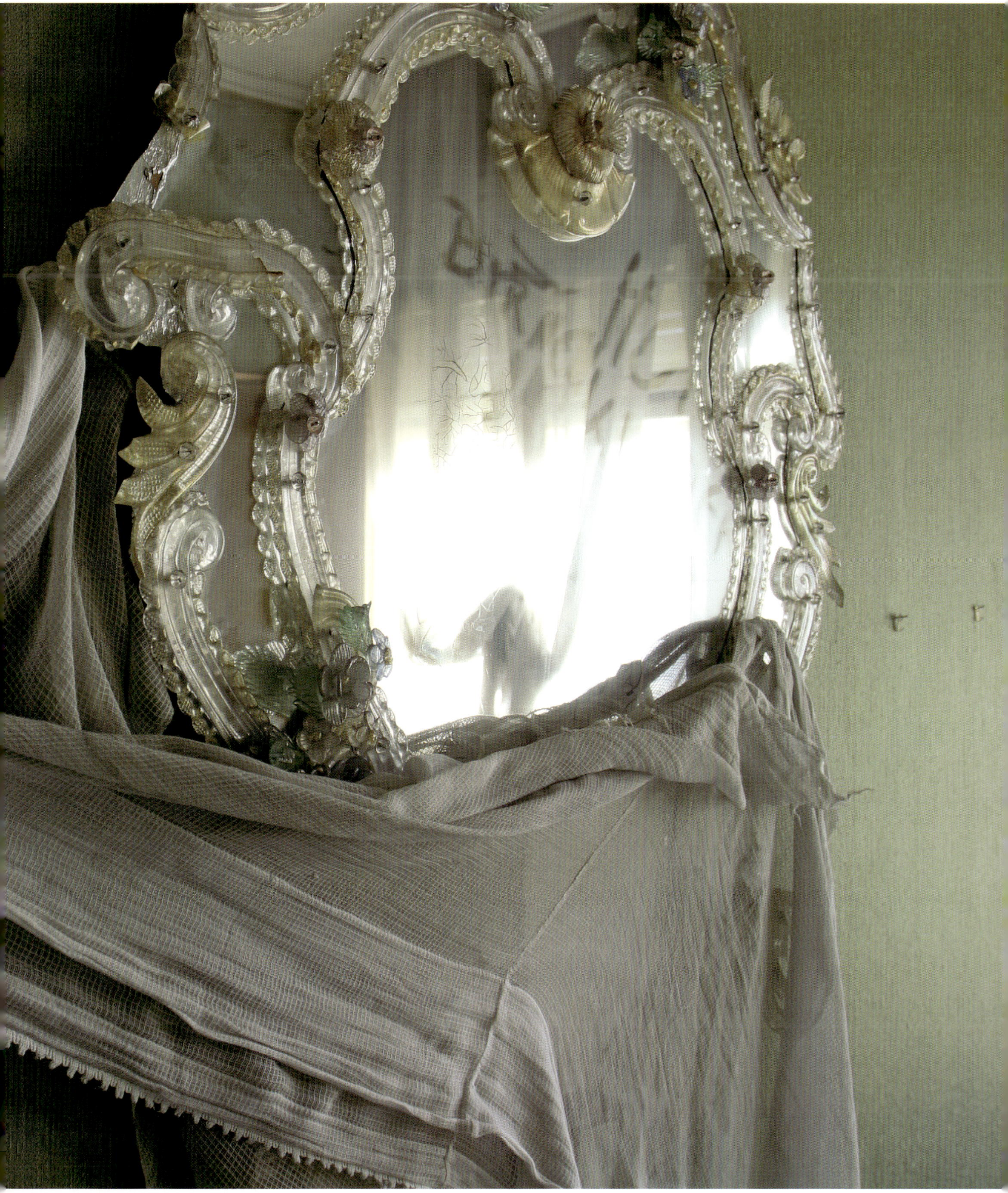

Checked Out – A Photographic Sketch Book   Matthias Dusini

For more than two years, Elisabeth Hölzl visited the abandoned Hotel Bristol in Merano. Her intention was not so much to soberly document the building, but rather to keep a diary of the relationship the artist developed to the mysterious place in the centre of her city. From close up, her camera brushes against the surfaces of the rooms and gets caught on details – the backs of chairs, mirrors, velvet curtains, or white covers. This closeness adds a sensual naturalness to her pictures, as though one could wipe the dust off the furniture with one's fingers. Traditional architectural photography is meant to document a building before it is occupied. Elisabeth Hölzl, however, shows a building that has been used up, as if she sought to keep it alive. Her pictures are advertisement photographs for a ruin, as it were. With Stanley Kubrick's movie *Shining,* abandoned hotels became a topos of the uncanny, a playground of cryptic imagination. In his book *The Architectural Uncanny* (1992), the American architectural theorist Anthony Vidler identified the uncanny as the constituting parameter of the modern understanding of space. Elisabeth Hölzl's photographs reverse the clearly established aura of such seemingly alien abodes. Rays of sunlight pierce the rooms, and an ocean of white furniture covers in a hall bathed in light gives the impression of a cheery revolution of ghosts. Compared to these pictures, the old advertisement postcards of the bar and dining hall of the former hotel look dull. Commercial pictures filter spots out of faces and cracks out of buildings, whereas the mimetic sensuality of these photographs is derived exactly from such blemishes.

During her photographic work for the book *Sinti und Roma – eine Spurensuche [Sinti and Roma – A Search for Traces]*, edited by E. Tauber, Elisabeth Hölzl visited the settlement of a Roma family in Bolzano for an extended period of time. Dealing with the portrayed persons day by day changes the quality of the camera. It is no longer a neutral machine that captures objects, but becomes witness to a relationship that evolves between the photographer and the Roma family. That is Elisabeth Hölzl's answer to the criticism of the ethnographic eye which claimed that it is not possible to record the symbolic systems of foreign cultures with supposed scientific neutrality. Her approach to Hotel Bristol follows the same logics of a self-reflective ethnographic eye. An abandoned hotel that lacks apparent architectural quality could be considered a synonym for a worthless object, bound to be destroyed with impunity. Elisabeth Hölzl conveys a symbolic meaning to these rooms that are destined for oblivion by underlining their patina as a special atmospheric quality. The German philosopher Gernot Böhme defines atmosphere as the prototype of an 'intermediate phenomenon', as something that lies between the subject and the object. Elisabeth Hölzl's photographs focus on the atmospheric value of these rooms, the form of which keep to the background for the sake of their charm.

In a first step, Elisabeth Hölzl gathered a collection of photographs; then she decided on the criteria for sorting and finally presenting her material. By the format and sequence of the selected photographs, the artist interprets the archive which bestows an order, but no semantic classification system. These formal decisions that determine even the layout of the book are influenced by the knowledge the artist acquired by lingering at the photographed place. What might have been an architectural documentation becomes the interpretation of a building. The mimetic effect of the enlarged individual picture forms a contrast to the series of pictures that communicate a structural message. In the book, she strings photographs of chairs together and creates the impression of serial monotony. Floor by floor, the same ground plan is repeated, and there is the same sequence of green, red, yellow, and purple painted rooms, so room number 210 is exactly underneath room number 310 and is identical with room number 410. Exclusiveness, not serial exchangeability, is what hotels promise. Therefore, the standardised cell structure of the building must be hidden from the eyes of its guests; only Elisabeth Hölzl's documentation makes it visible.

The photographic series also shows the progressive demolishing of the hotel, the chronological order of its gradual divestment. Little by little, the carcass emerges, and the tectonics beneath the luxurious texture of the early years, aesthetically heightened by advertisements and newspaper reports, are exposed. Bit by bit, the objects disappear from the rooms; a glass leaves behind a stain on a tabletop, and a bright spot on the wall marks the place where there once hung a mirror. In the end, the photographs will be the only remaining traces of the building. The camera freezes a process of measured dematerialisation which, before it has ended, confers a new meaning to architecture. That becomes particularly evident with the heart of the hotel, the generous pool landscape on the roof. The empty pool and the structures with their slender pillars that have nearly fallen into disrepair add an almost ritual meaning to the site, as if an archaeological excavation would take place here and a holy shrine or temple would eventually be unearthed.

In spring 2006, the artist hung posters showing the interior of Hotel Bristol in the streets of Merano to attract attention to a building that had always remained a foreign object to the locals. Just before the hotel was to be demolished, the posters triggered a loud "Why?" In German-speaking territories, postmodern architecture in the last third of the twentieth century was defined by preserving historical city centres. In his book *L'architettura della città* (1966), Aldo Rossi criticised the total planning of modern urban development and gave emphasis to the identity-forming value of historical monuments. Even the architecture of high modernity is now taking on a memorial status. But what about buildings that are not included in the catalogue of cultural heritage? Post-war architecture is in a difficult position, as far as that is concerned. The unloved Hotel Bristol has now disappeared like a guest who came unasked and stayed too long. Nobody shed any tears over the thermal spring complex S.A.L.V.A.R. either, a far more demanding architectural project that was realised by Willi Gutweniger in 1972 and was demolished a few years ago. It, too, was documented by Elisabeth Hölzl.

In tourist regions, architecture has always been particularly worn out by commercially exploitable cycles of innovation. Bristol as well as the thermal springs stood where there were once grand hotels. The functionalist programme of modernity neglected the fact that the pictorial meaning overshadows the meaning of the tectonic structure, and that becomes evident here. Buildings are designed as strong images that must be replaced by others as soon as they have lost their signal character; Las Vegas is the best-known example for that. They are like old ocean liners – no one would bother restoring or converting them. *Usa e getta:* after they have been used, ships become scrap metal, and hotels are gutted and torn down. Elisabeth Hölzl counters this consumerist logic of our times by a contemplative occupation of space. In doing so, she does not call for the rescue of a building, but confines herself to the gesture of showing. She approaches the hotel as though it were a stranded whale, the looming death of which she cannot deny. Her emphatic photographs indicate that a city that regards its architecture as an inert structural mass forsakes its identity.

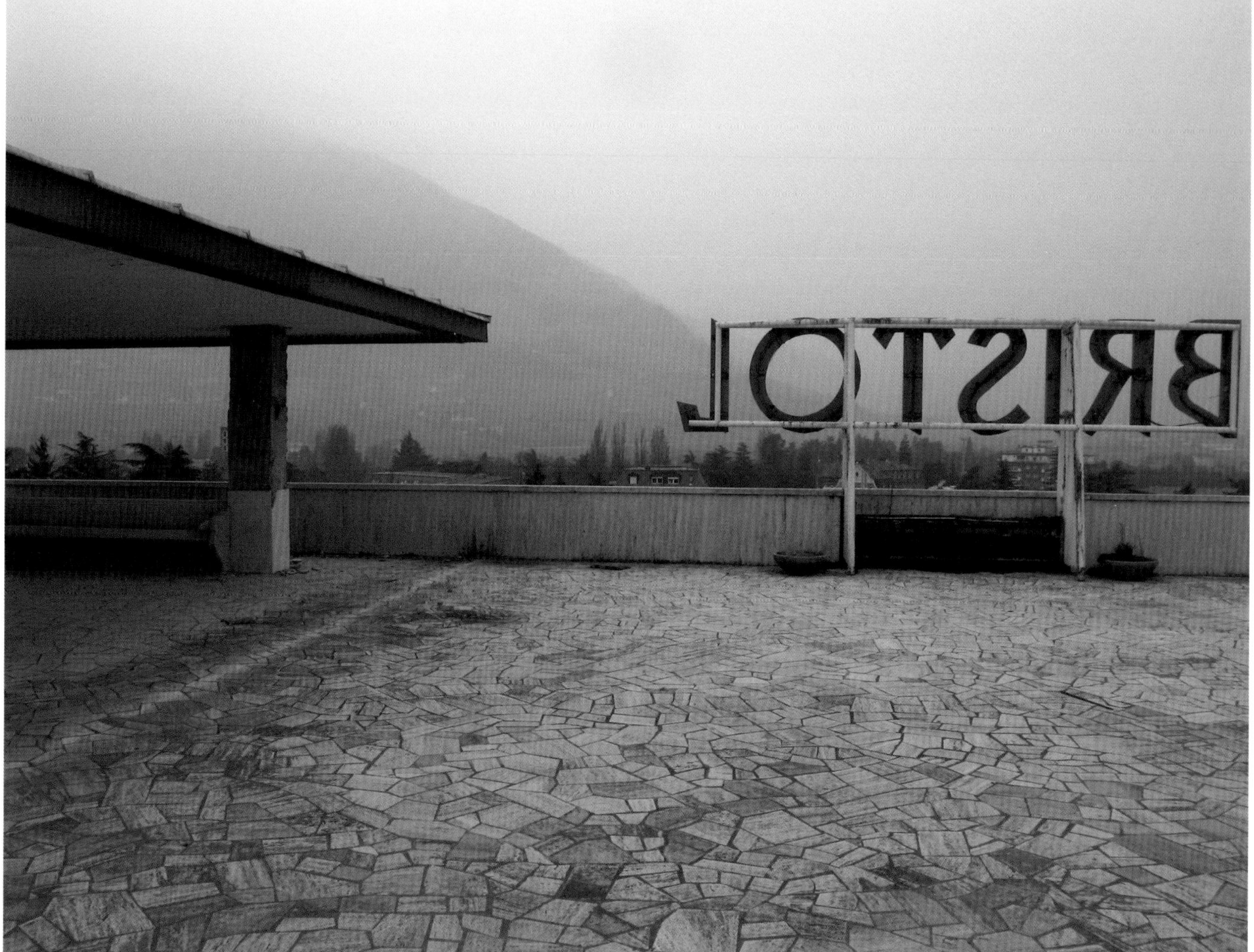
BRISTOL

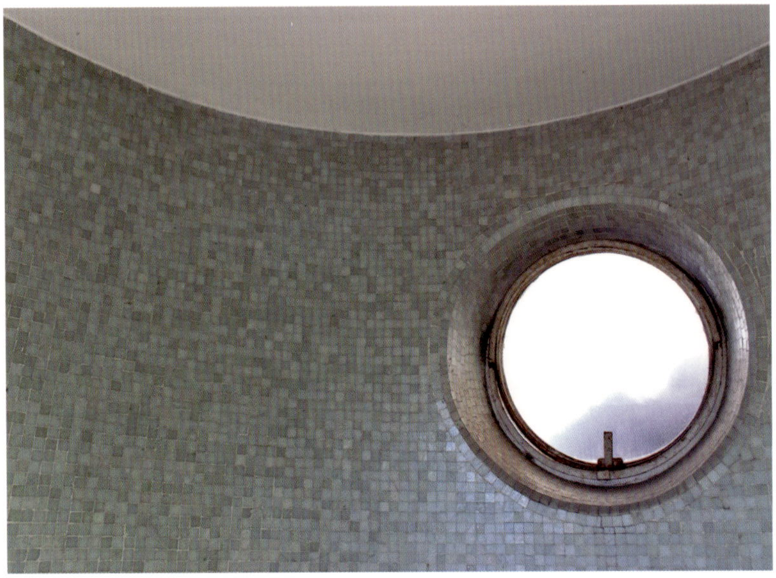

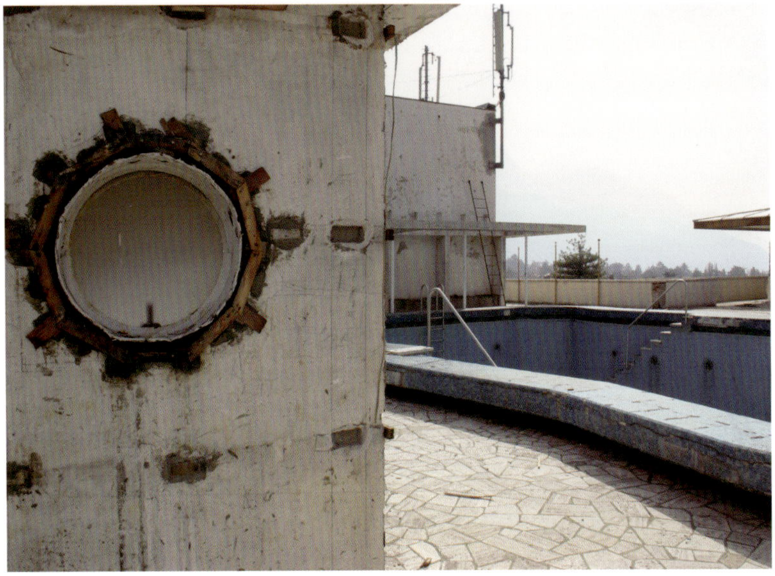

53

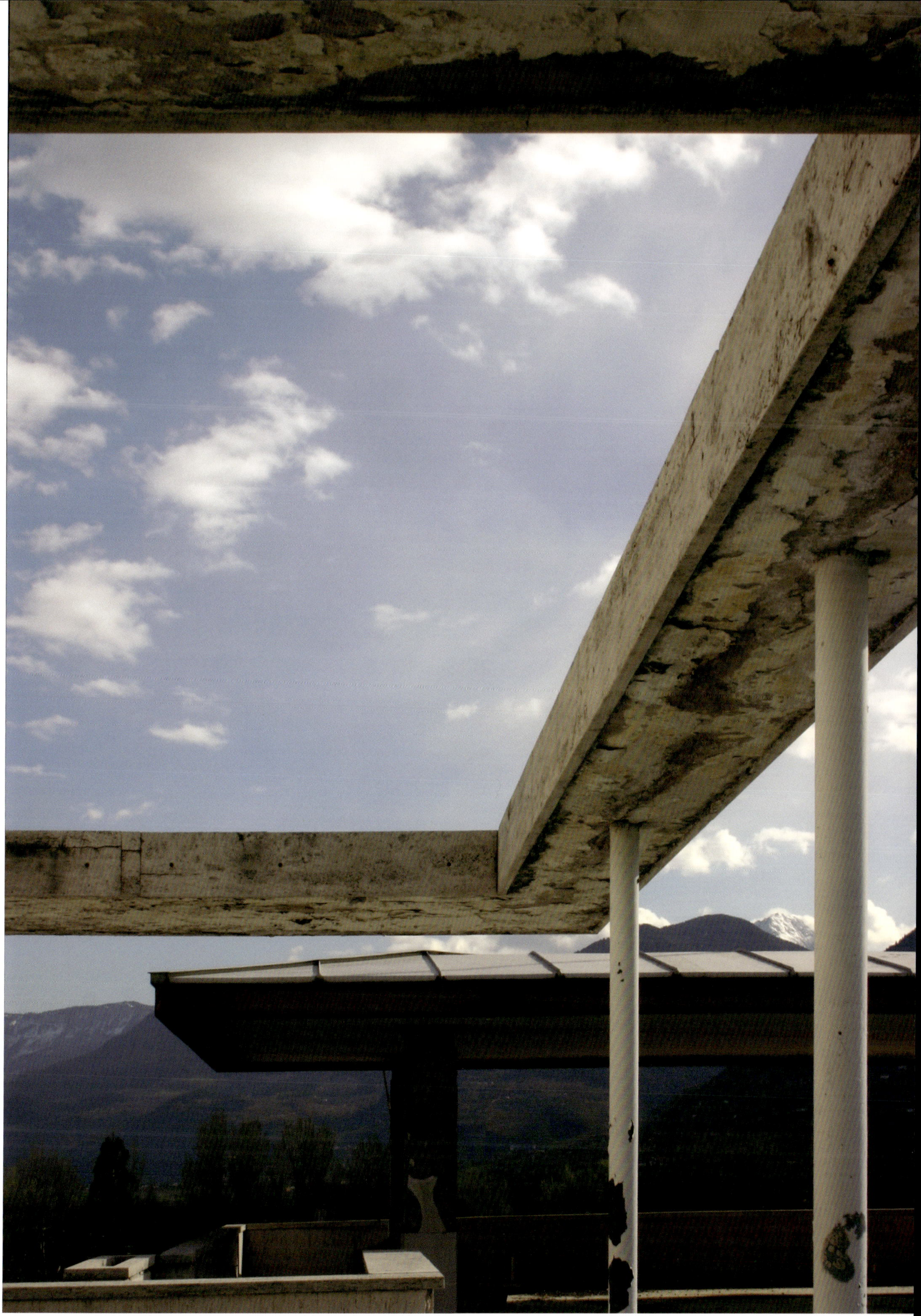

56

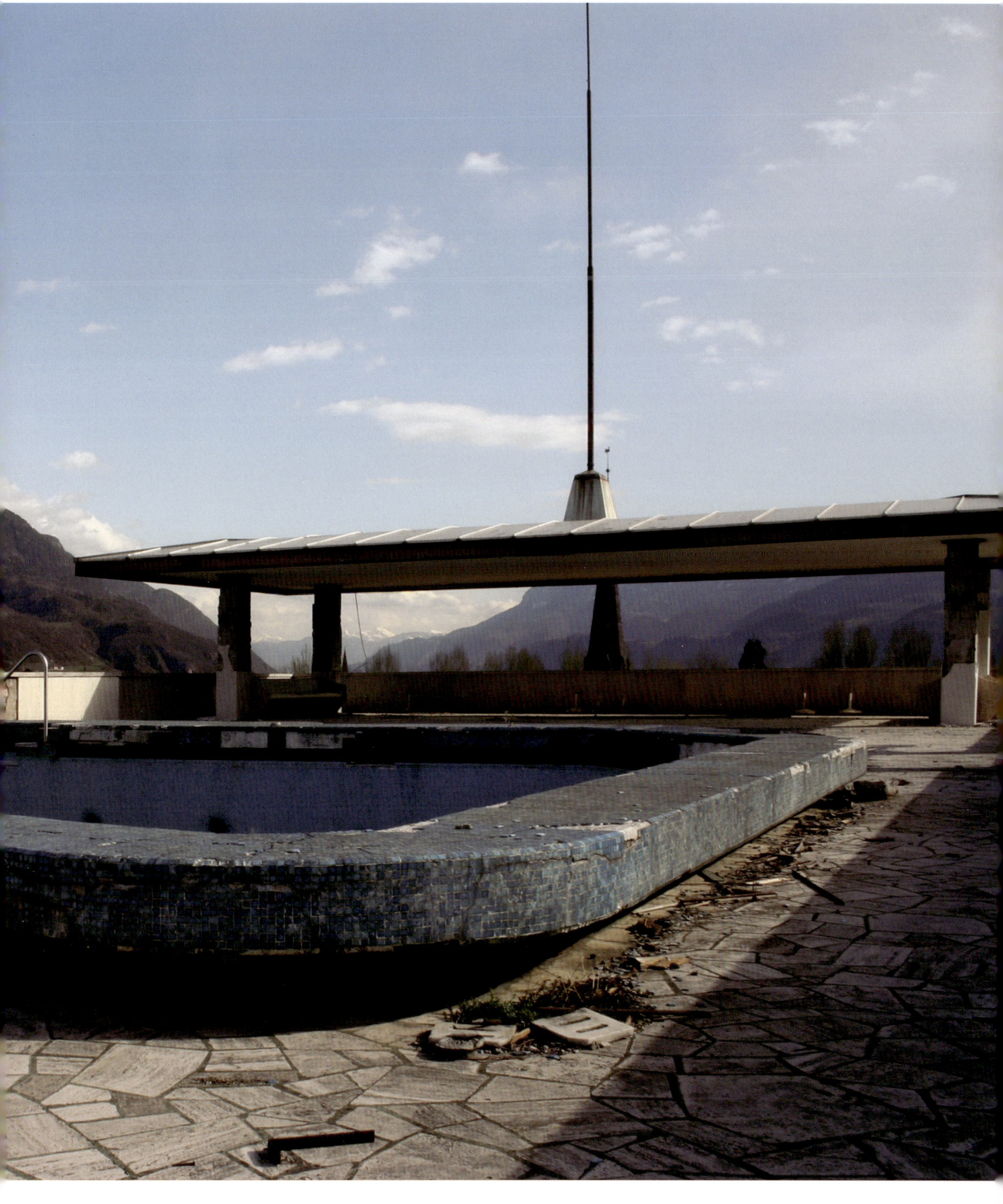

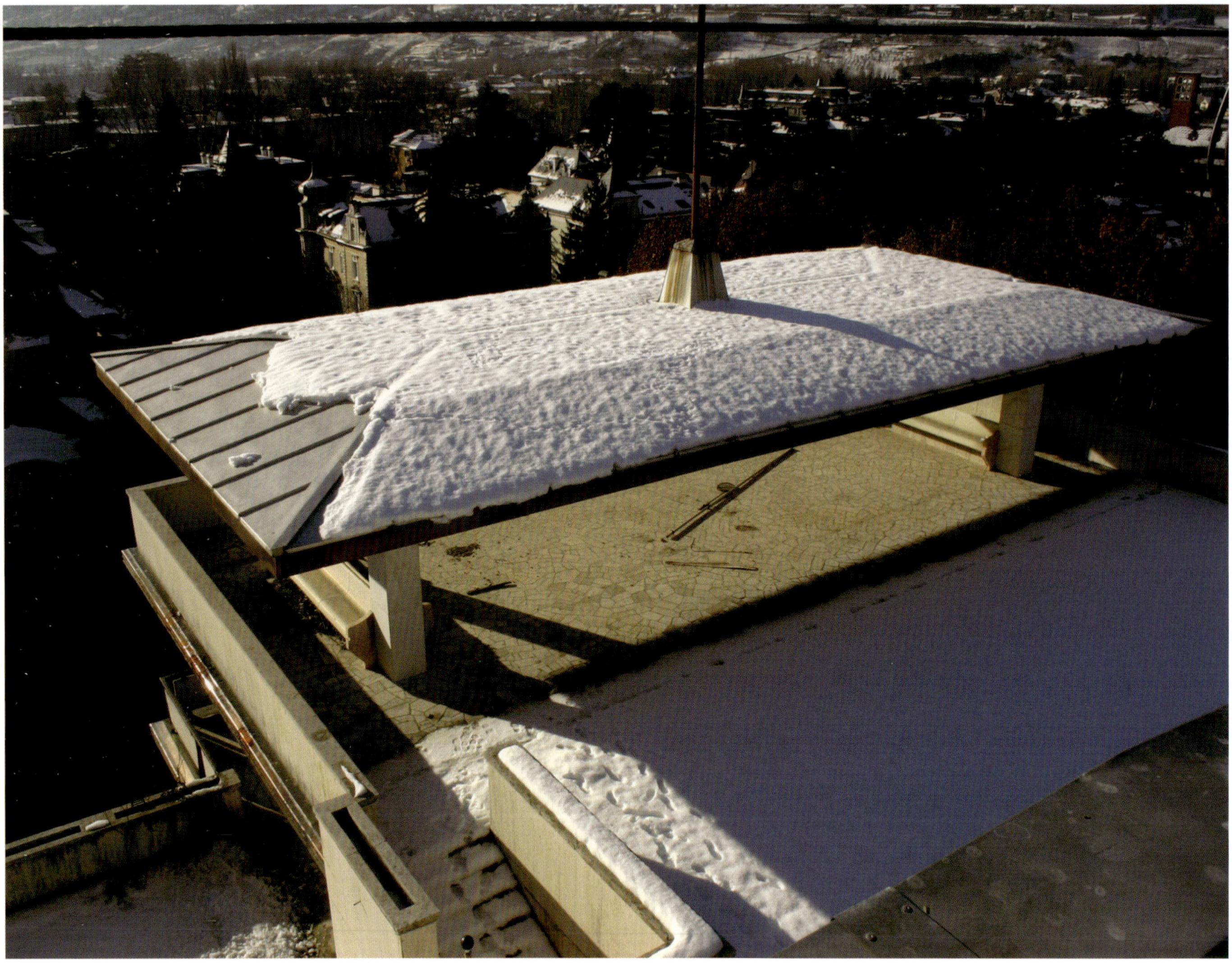

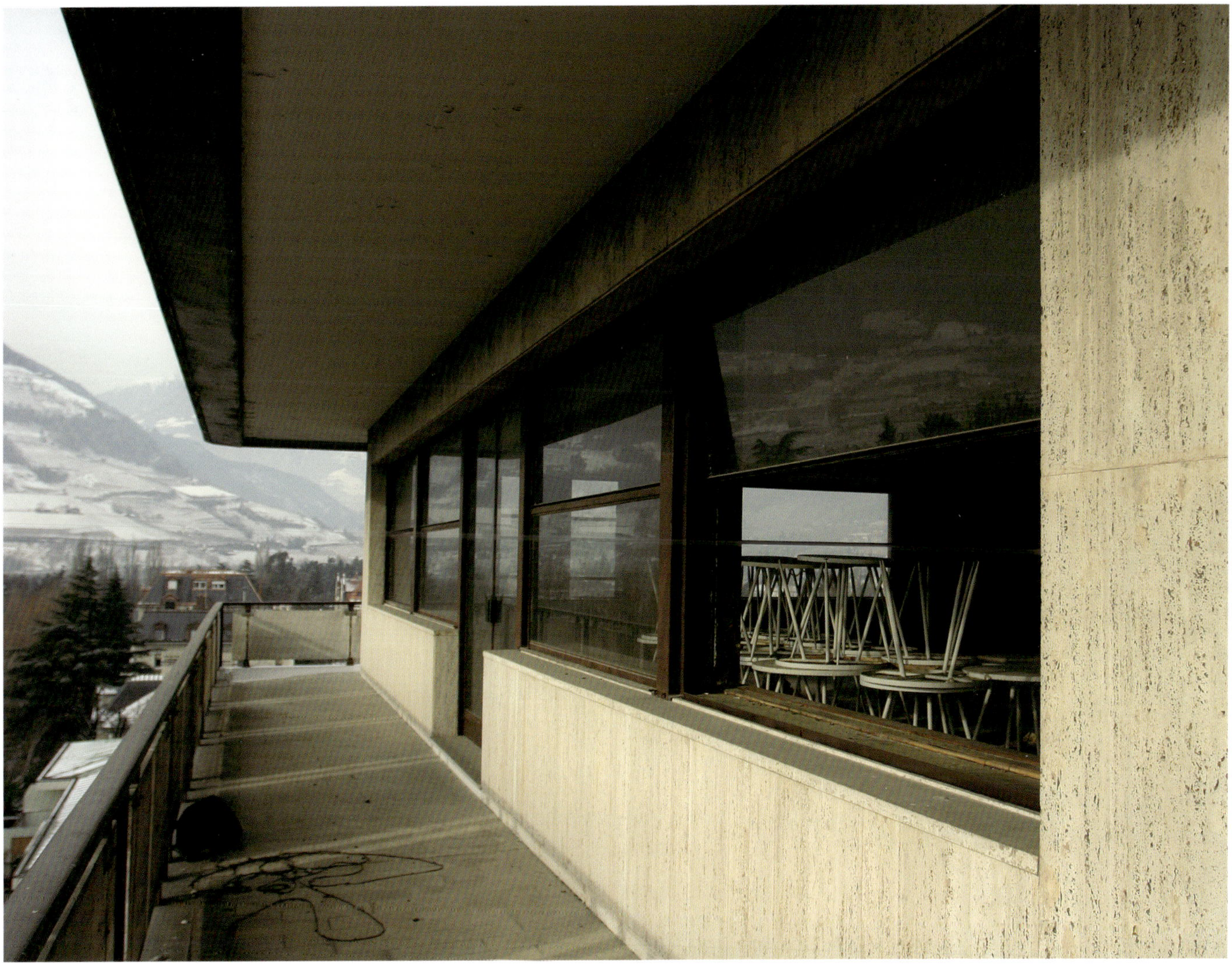

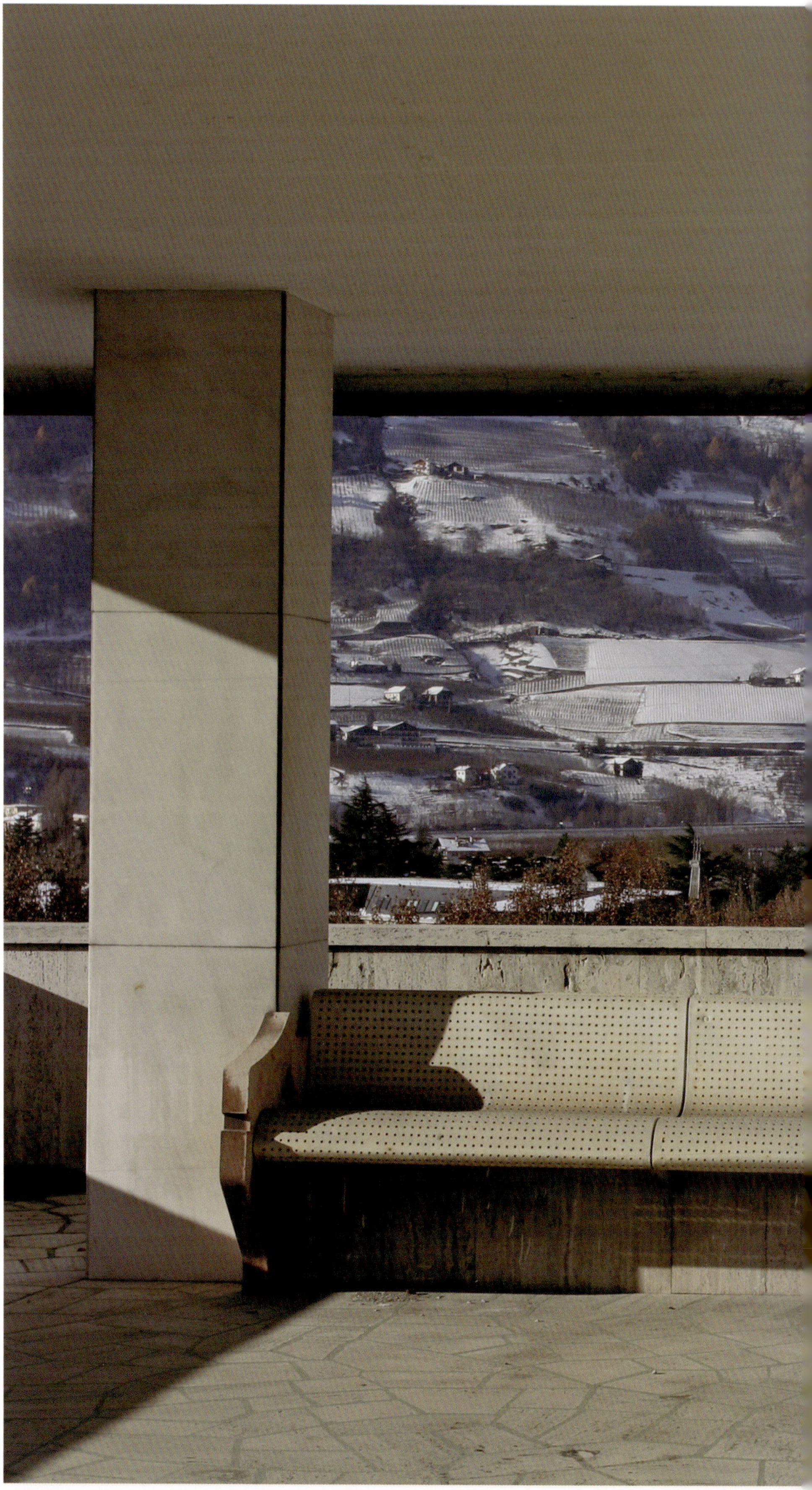

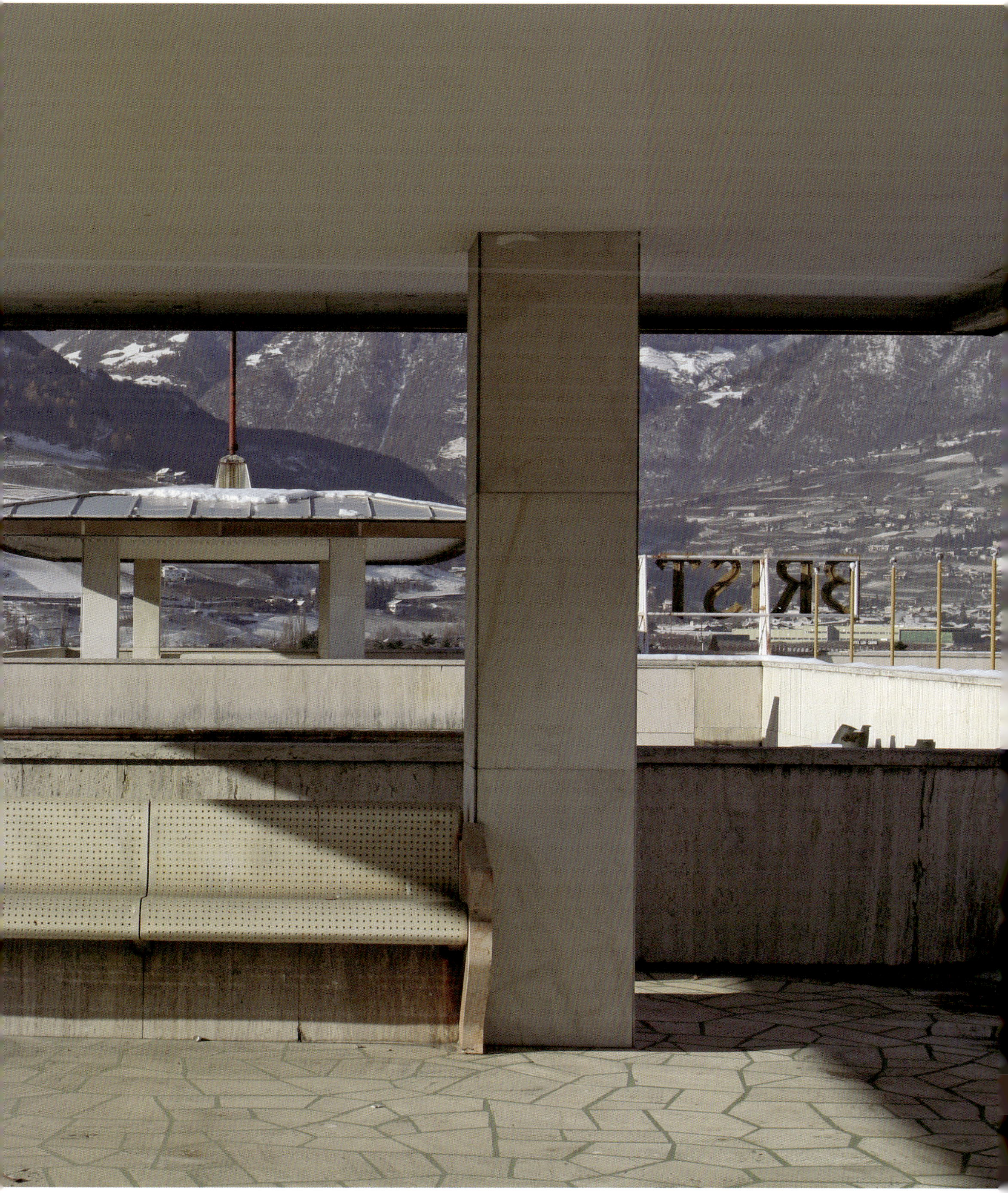

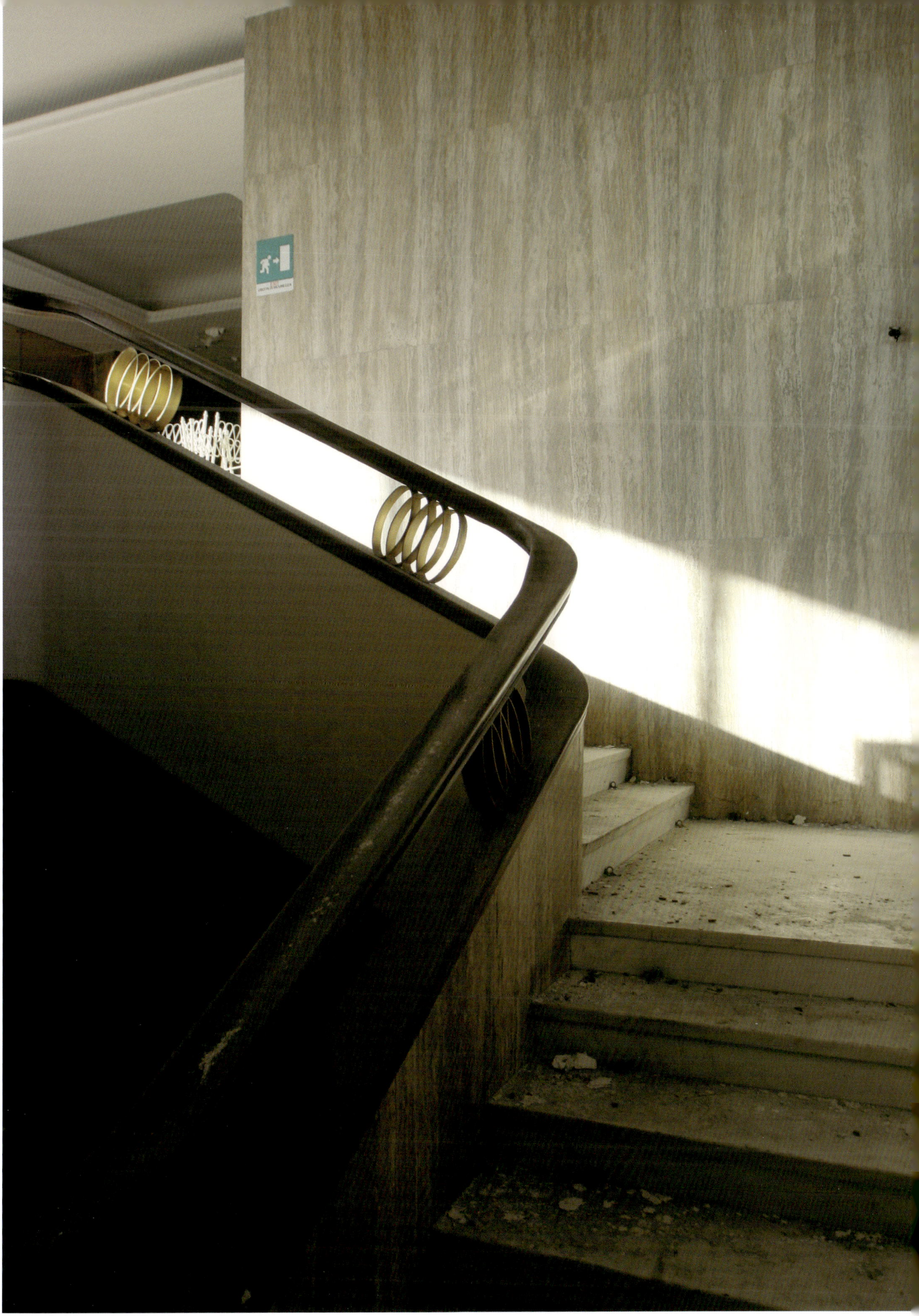

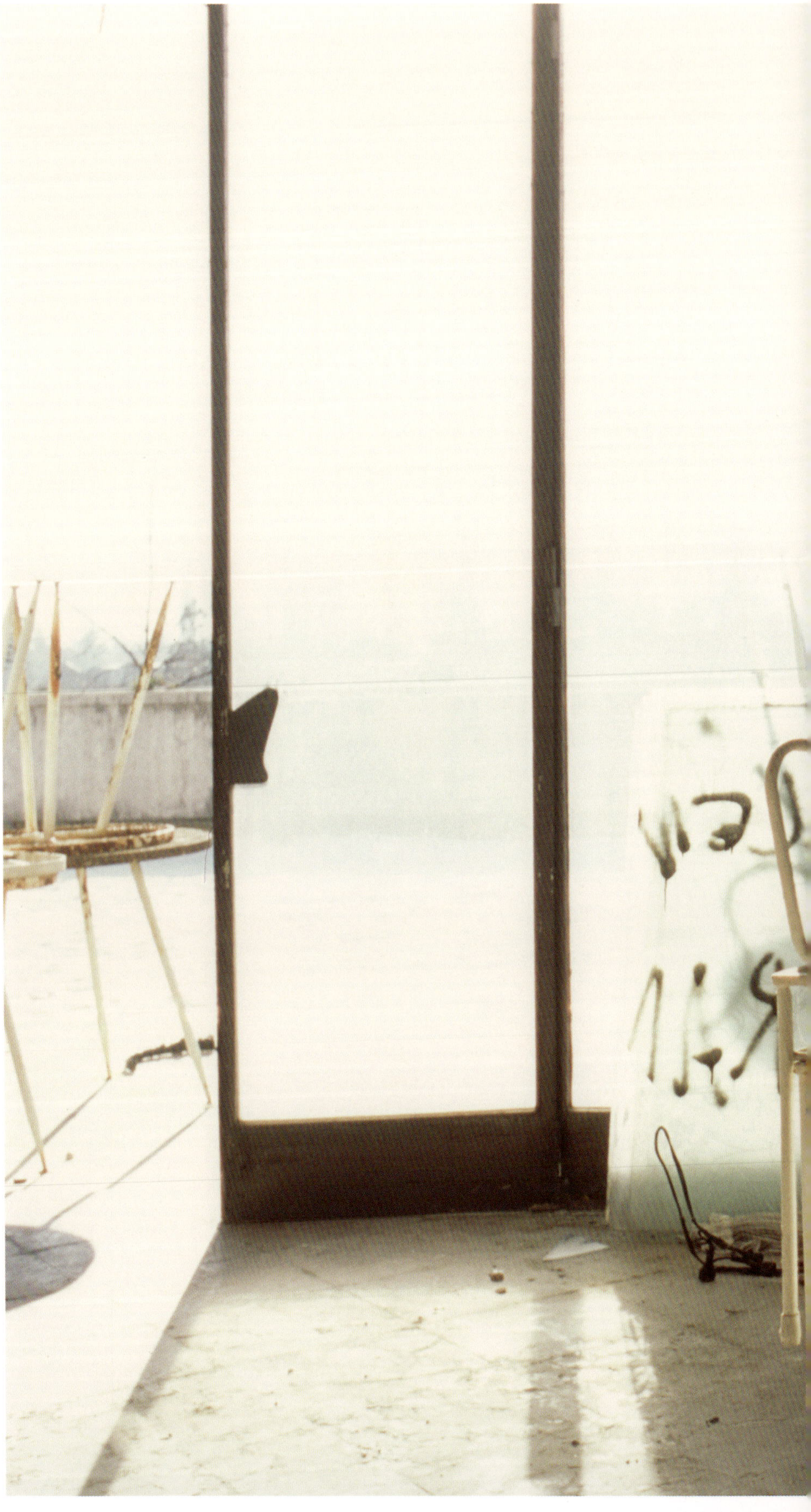

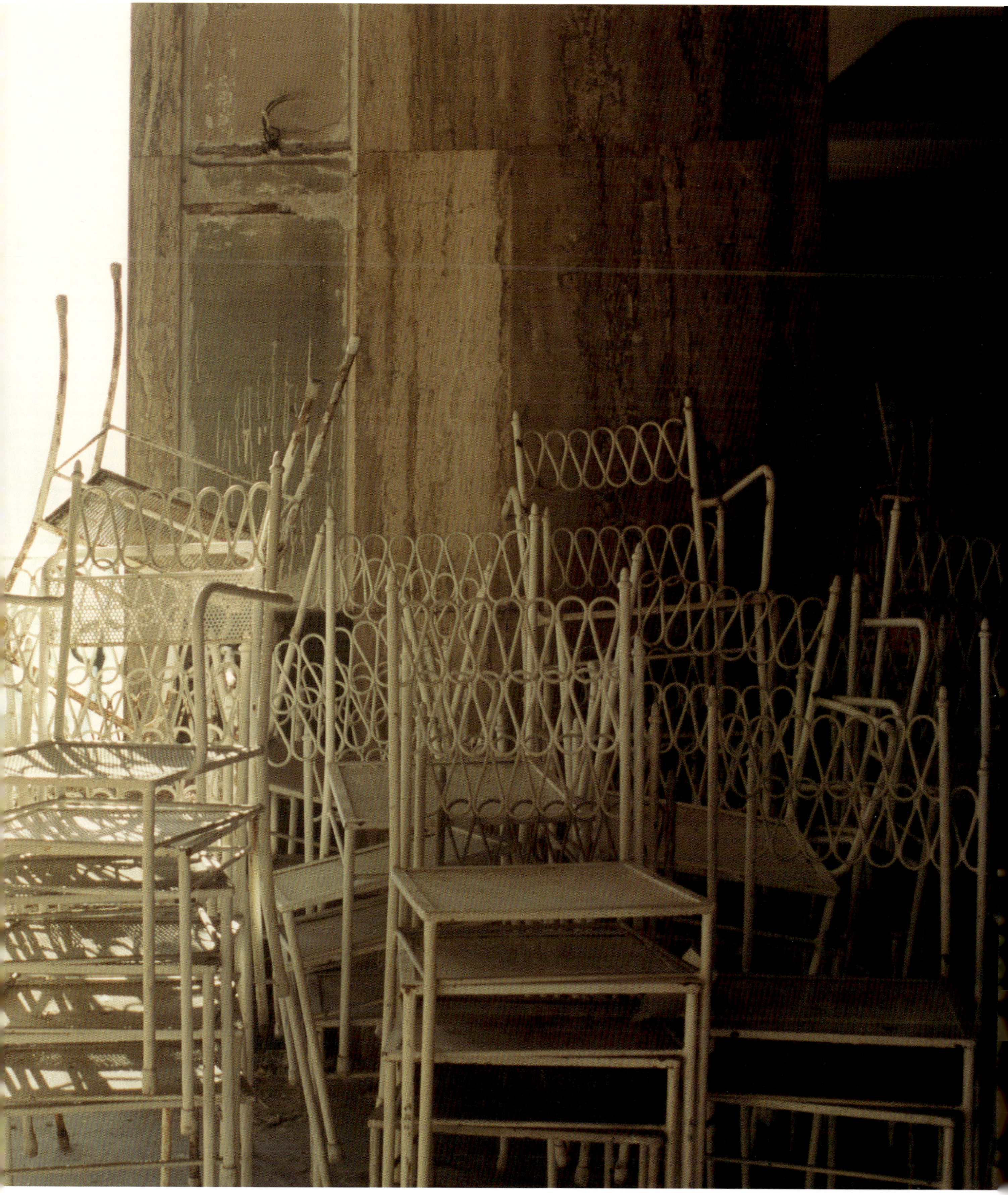

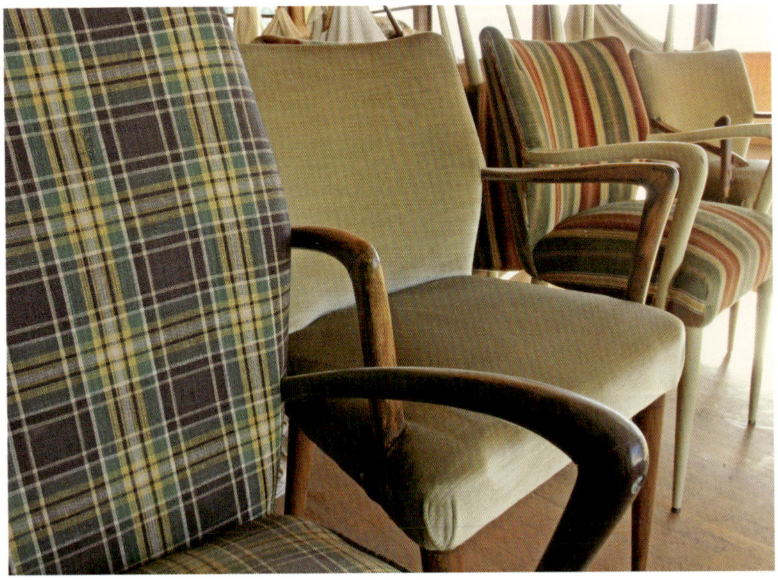

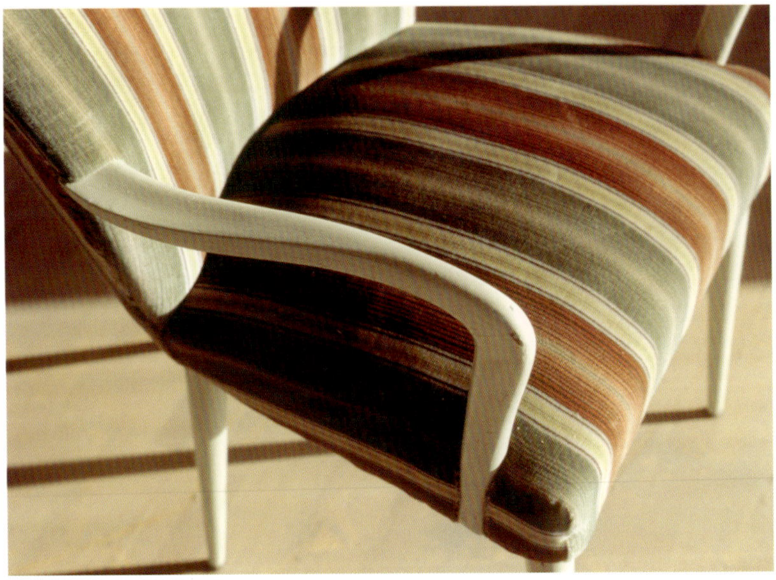

67

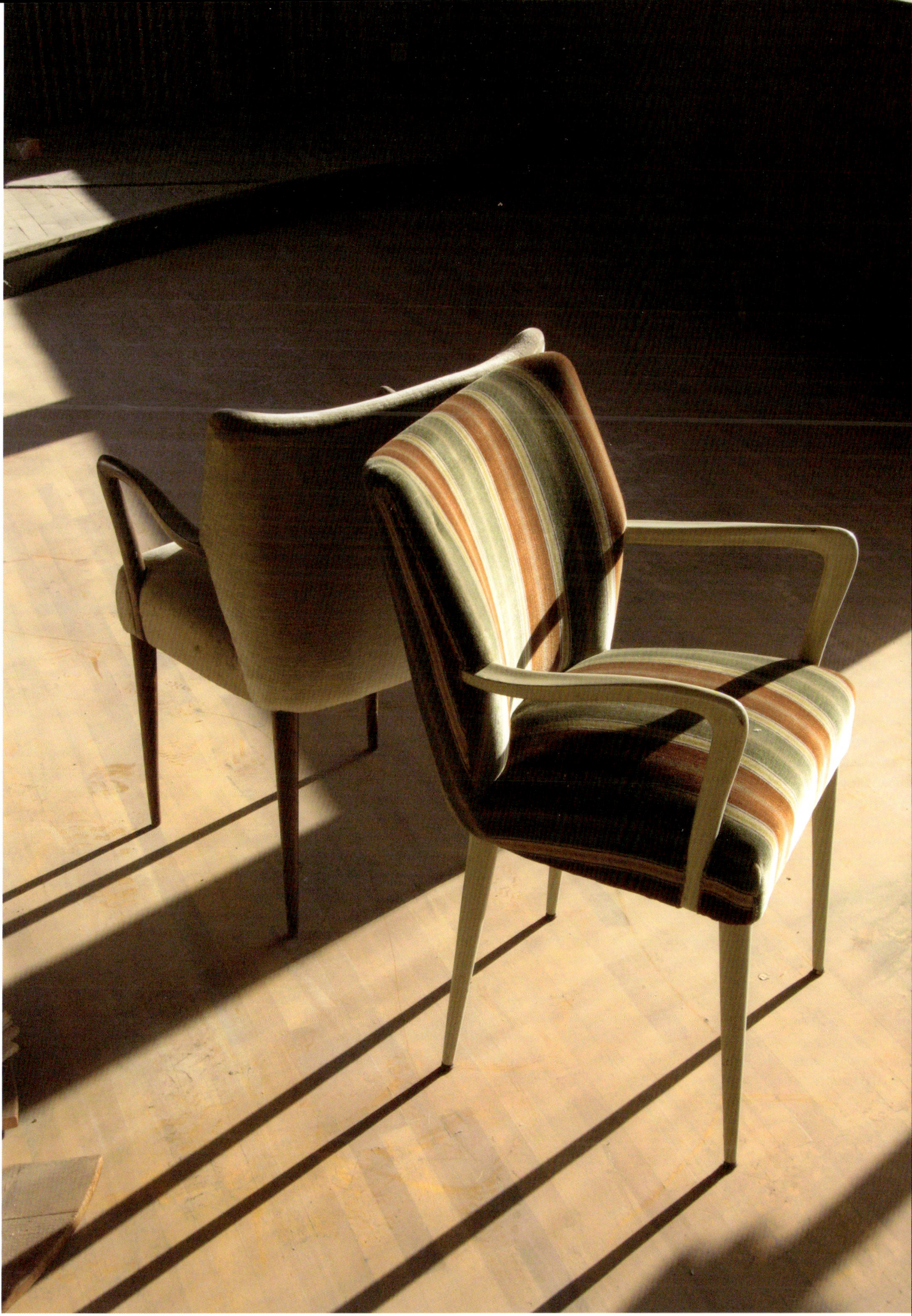

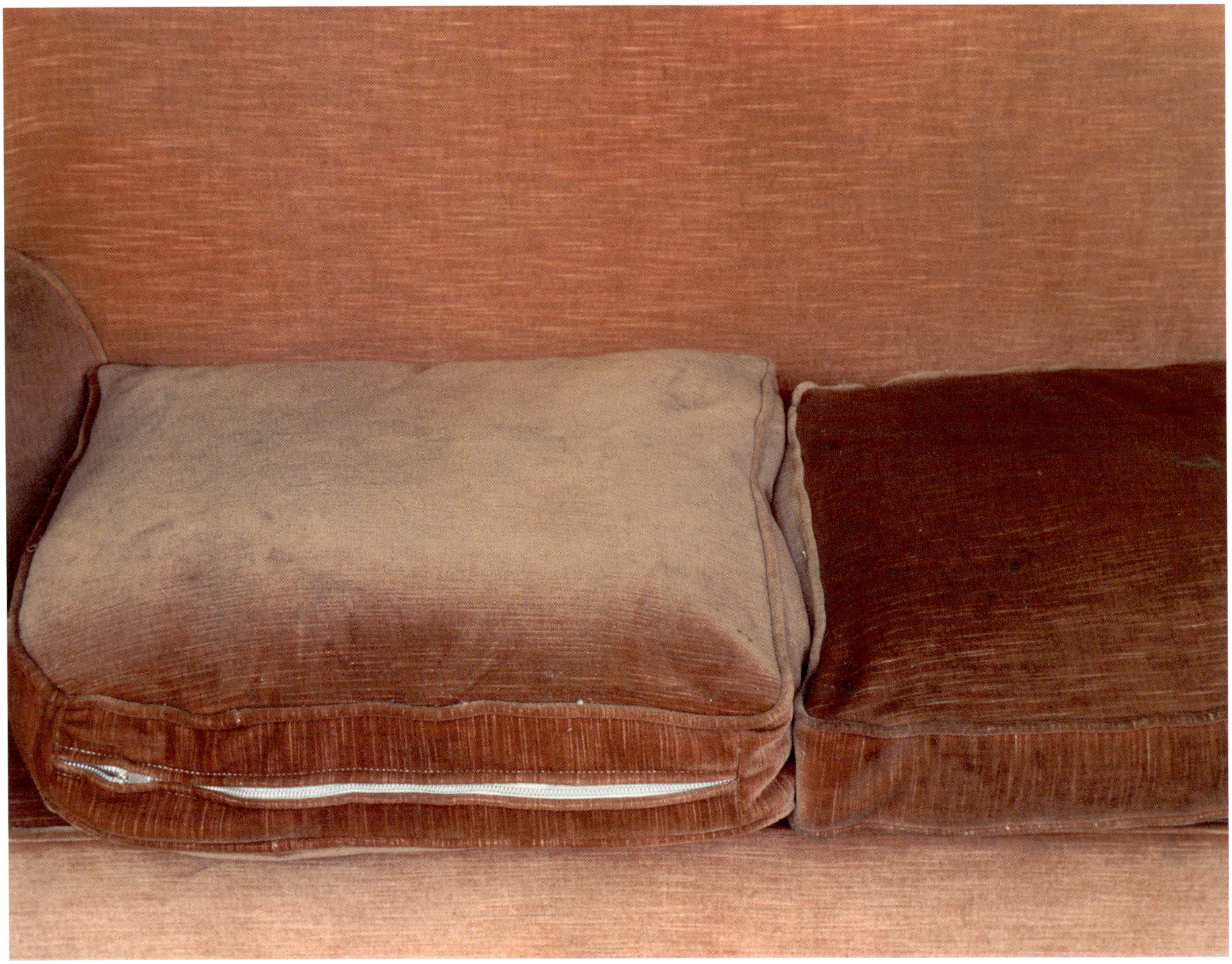

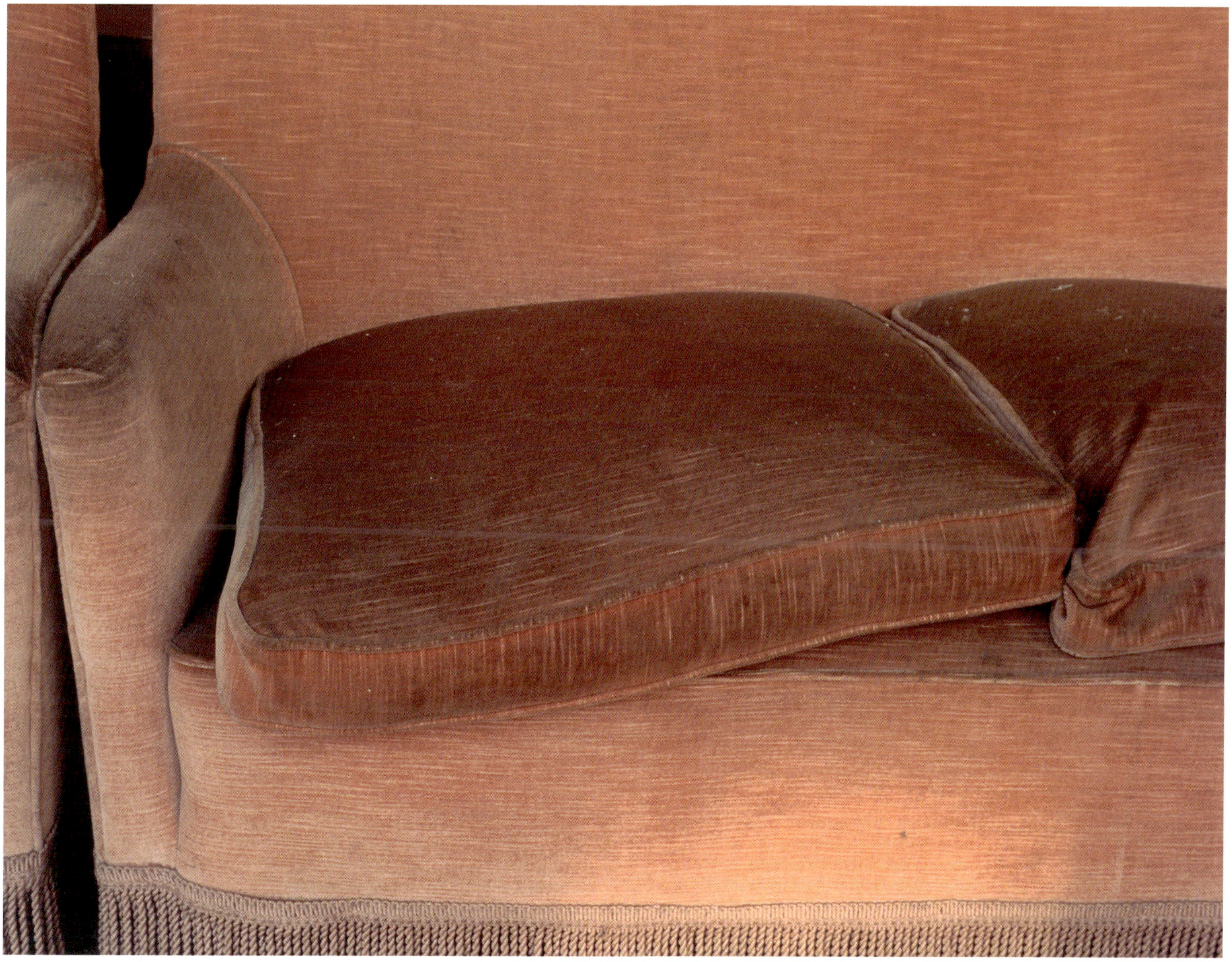

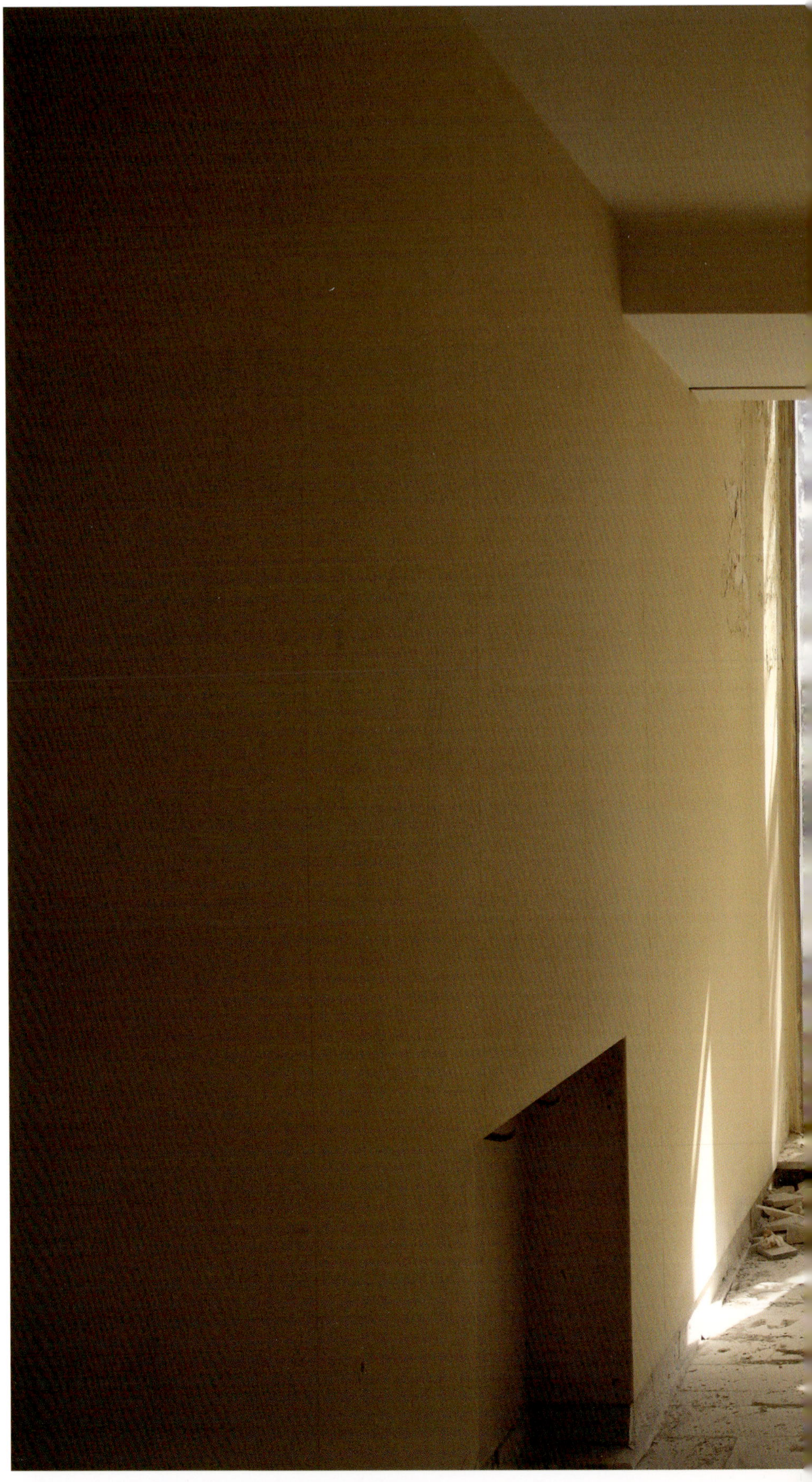

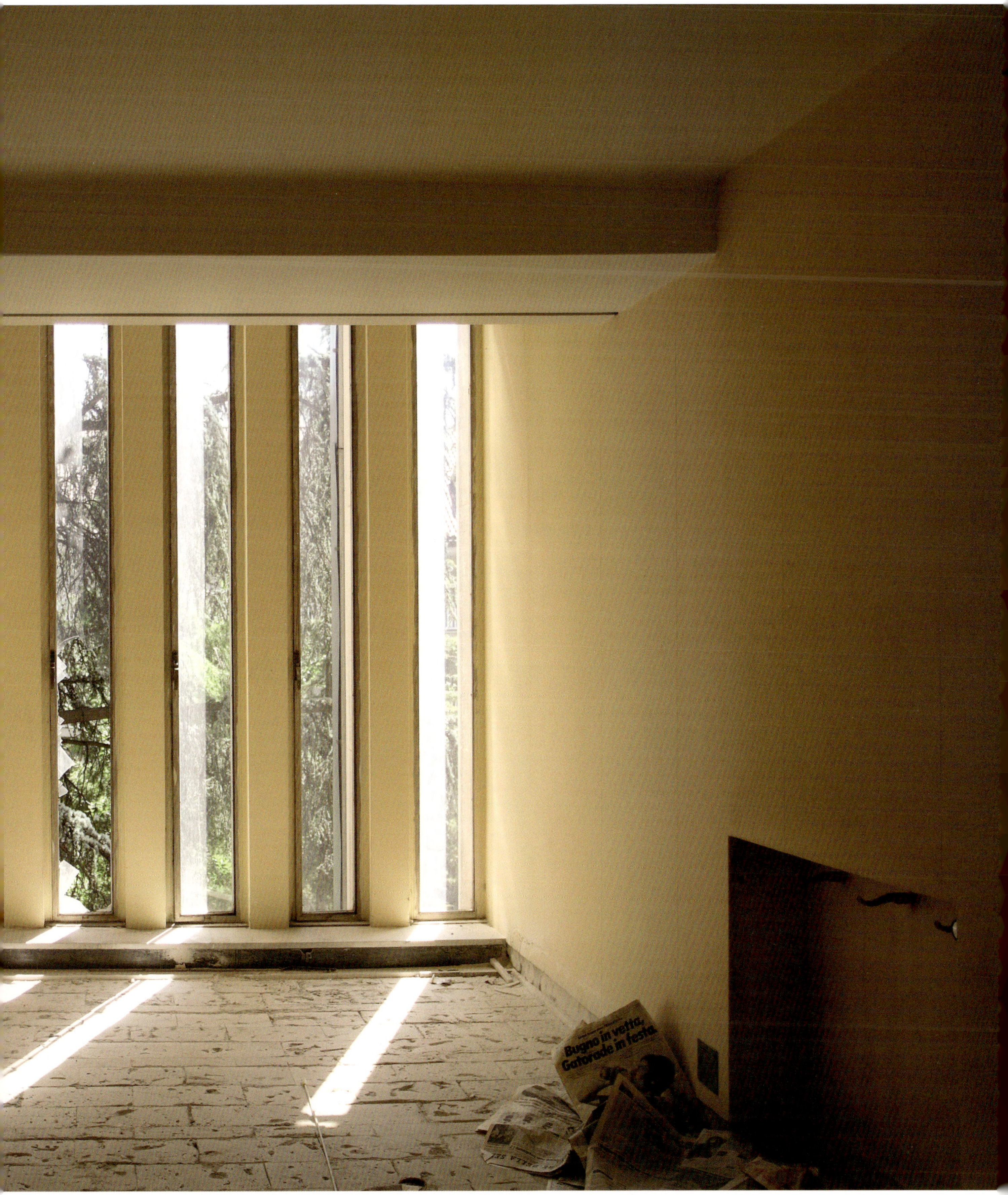
Bugno in vetta,
Gatorade in festa

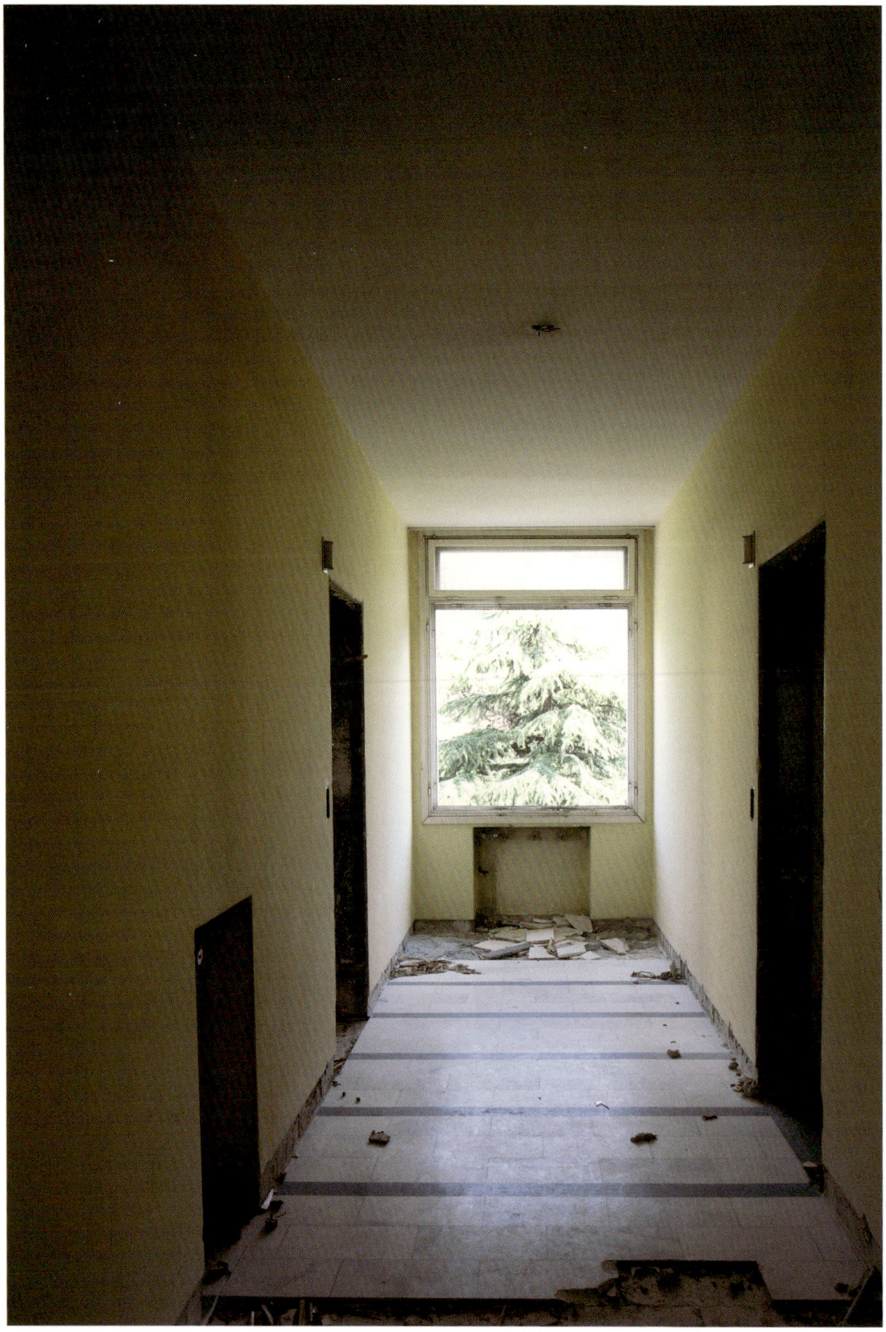

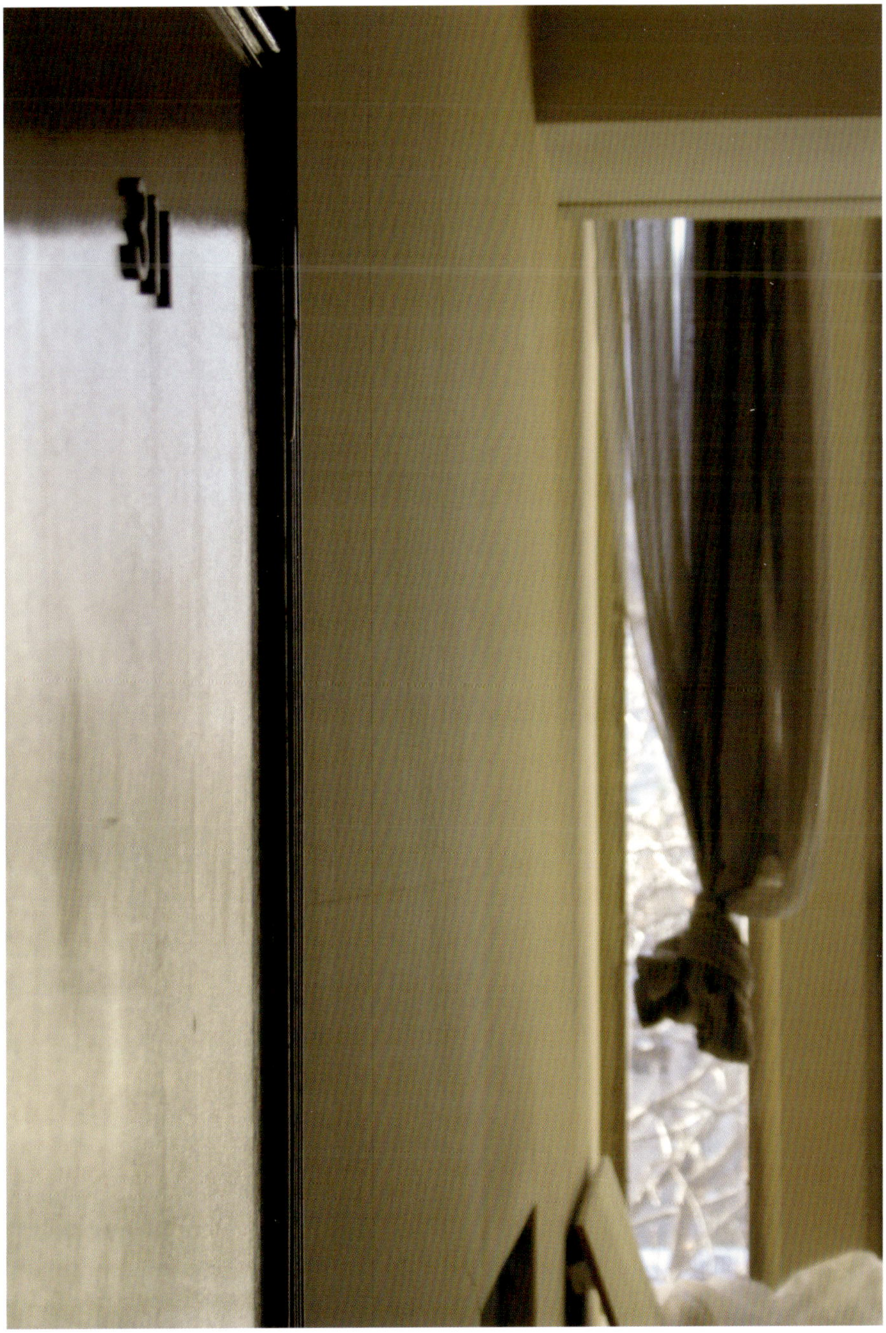

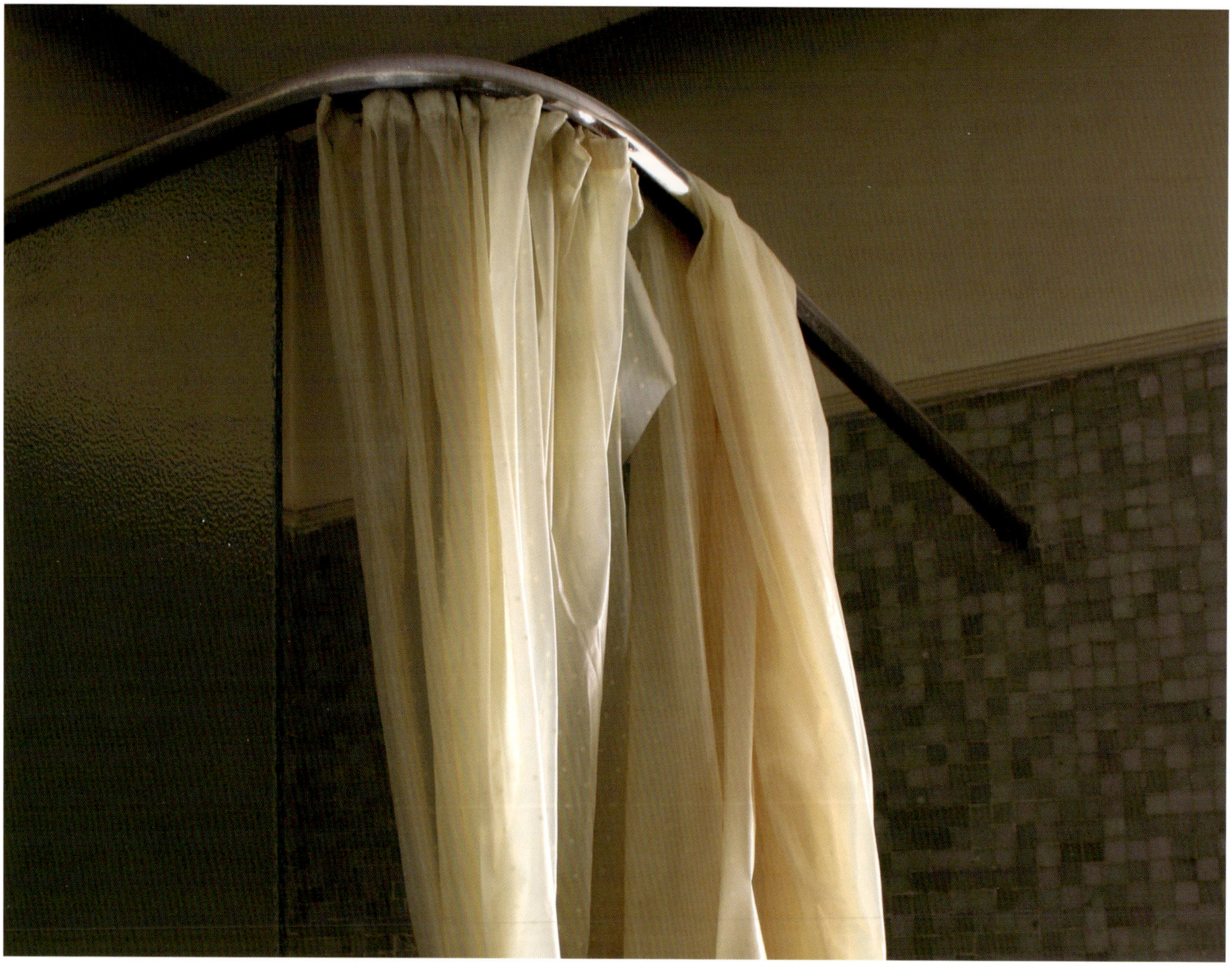

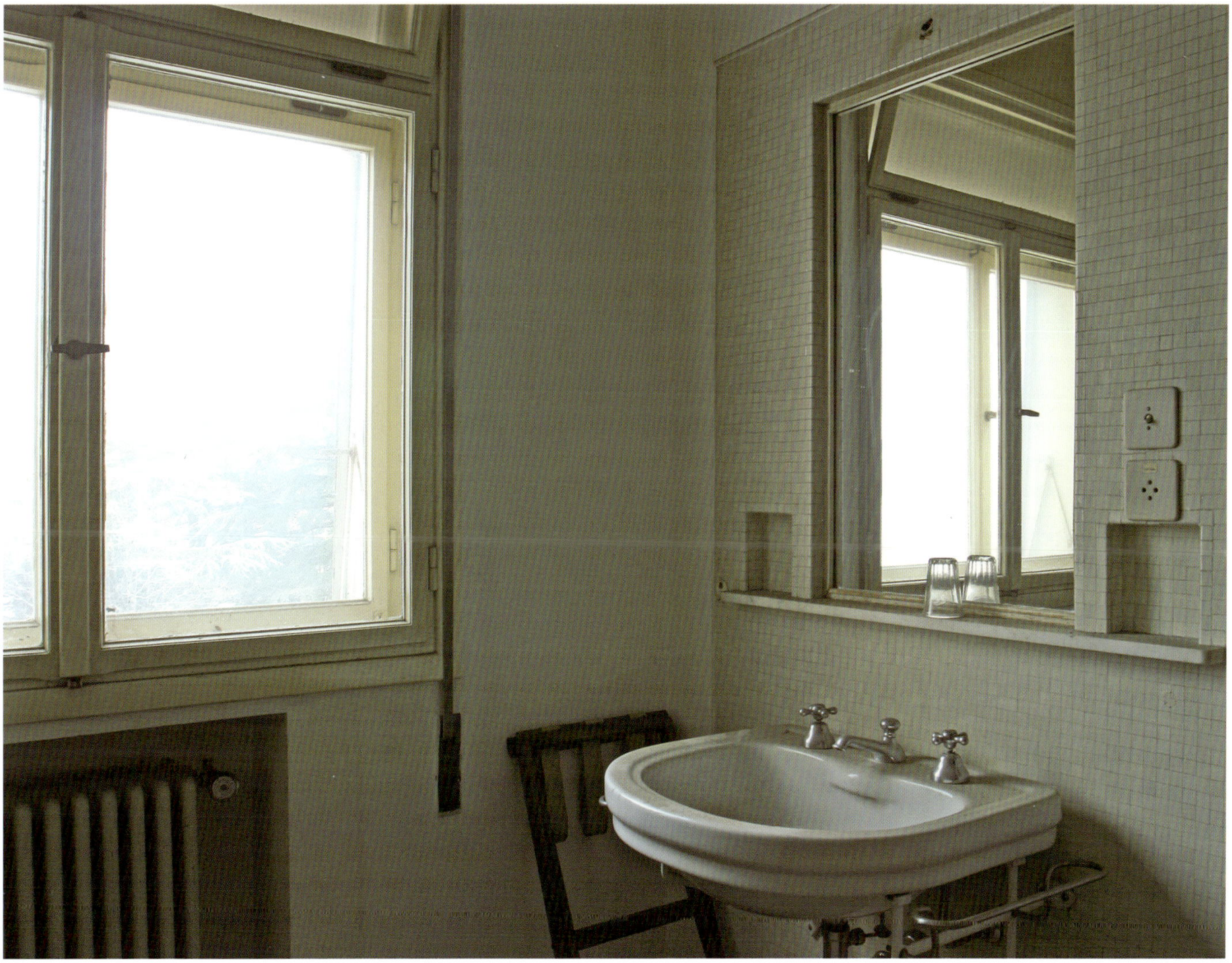

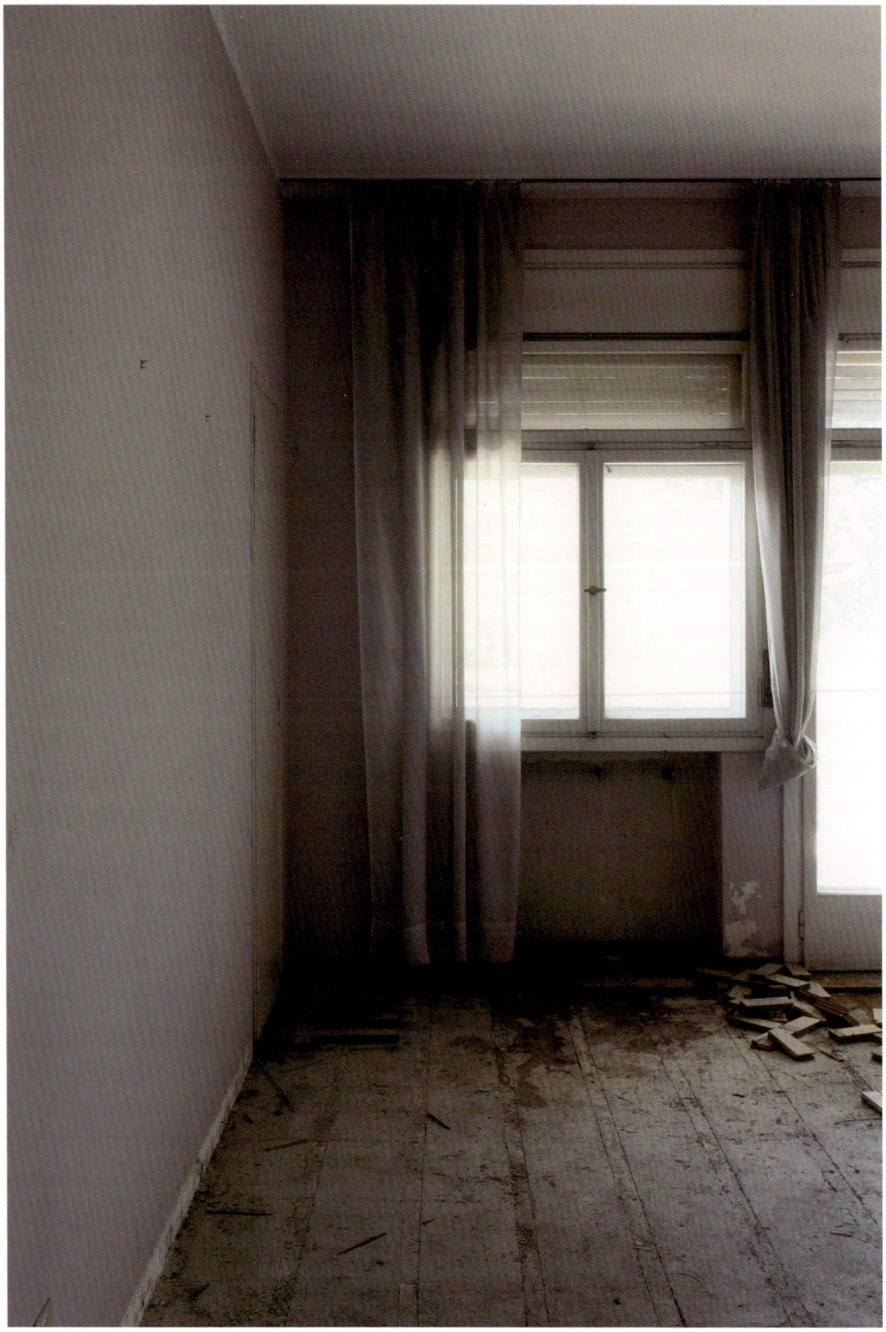

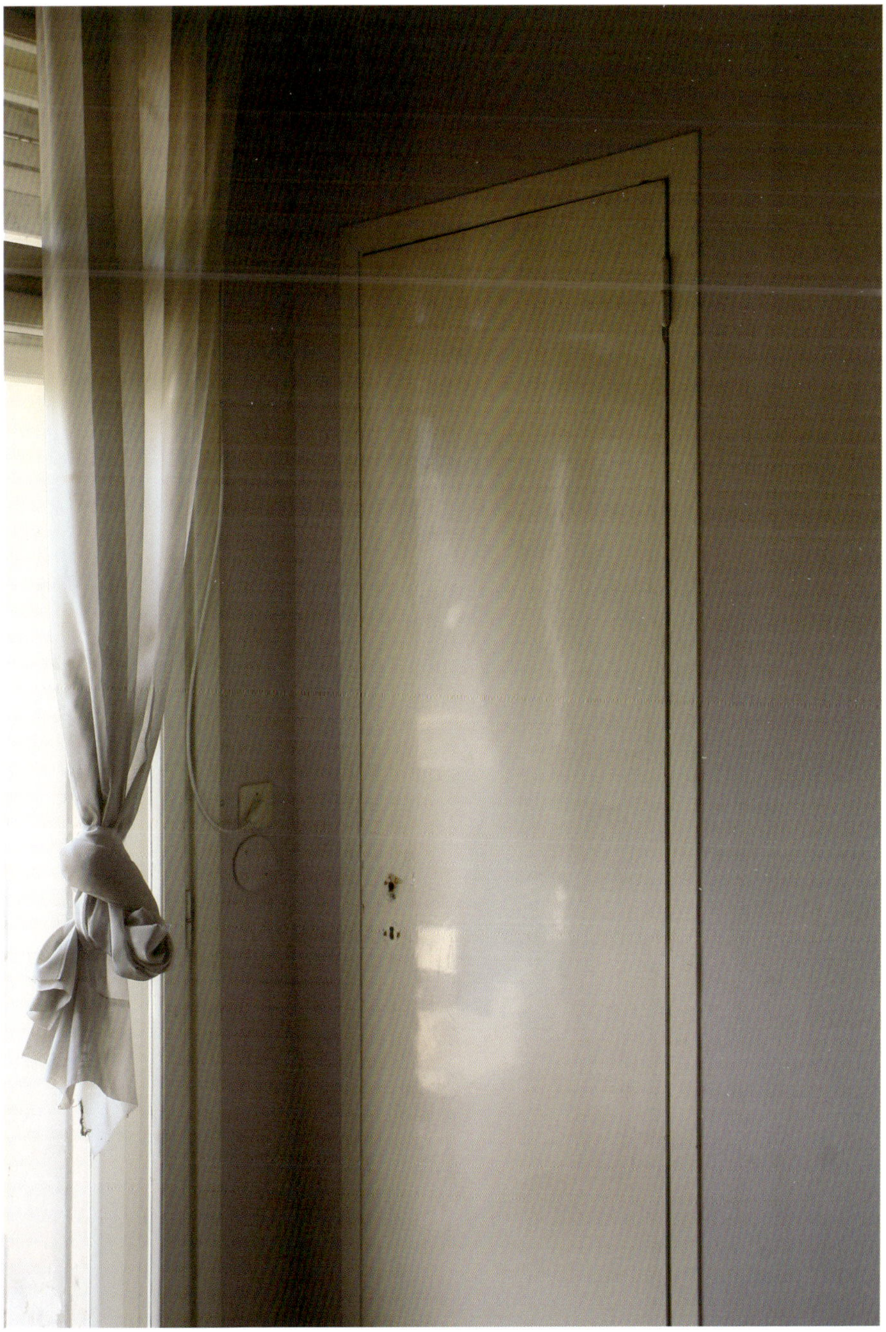

LONDRA
PARIGI
BERLINO
VIENNA

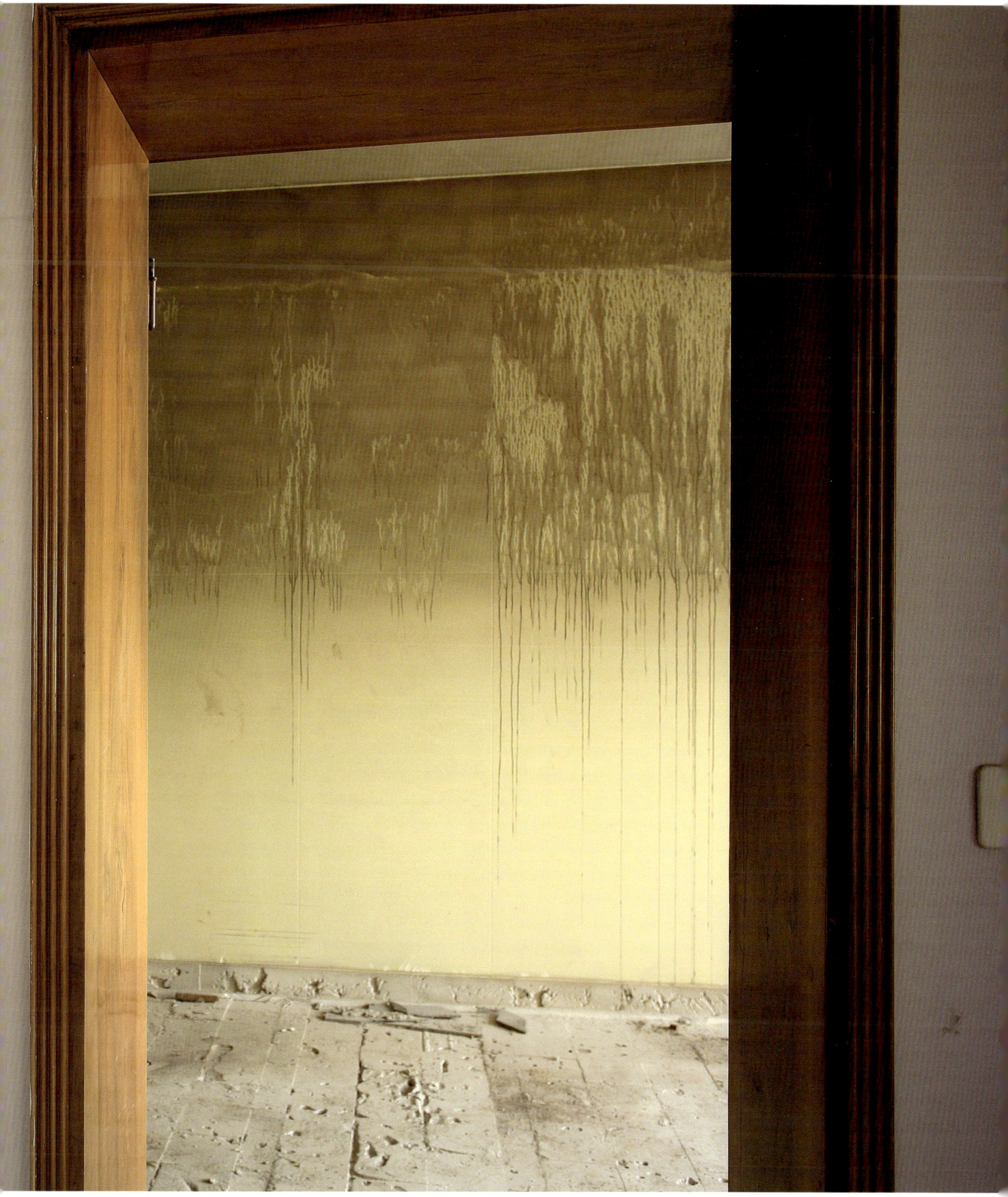

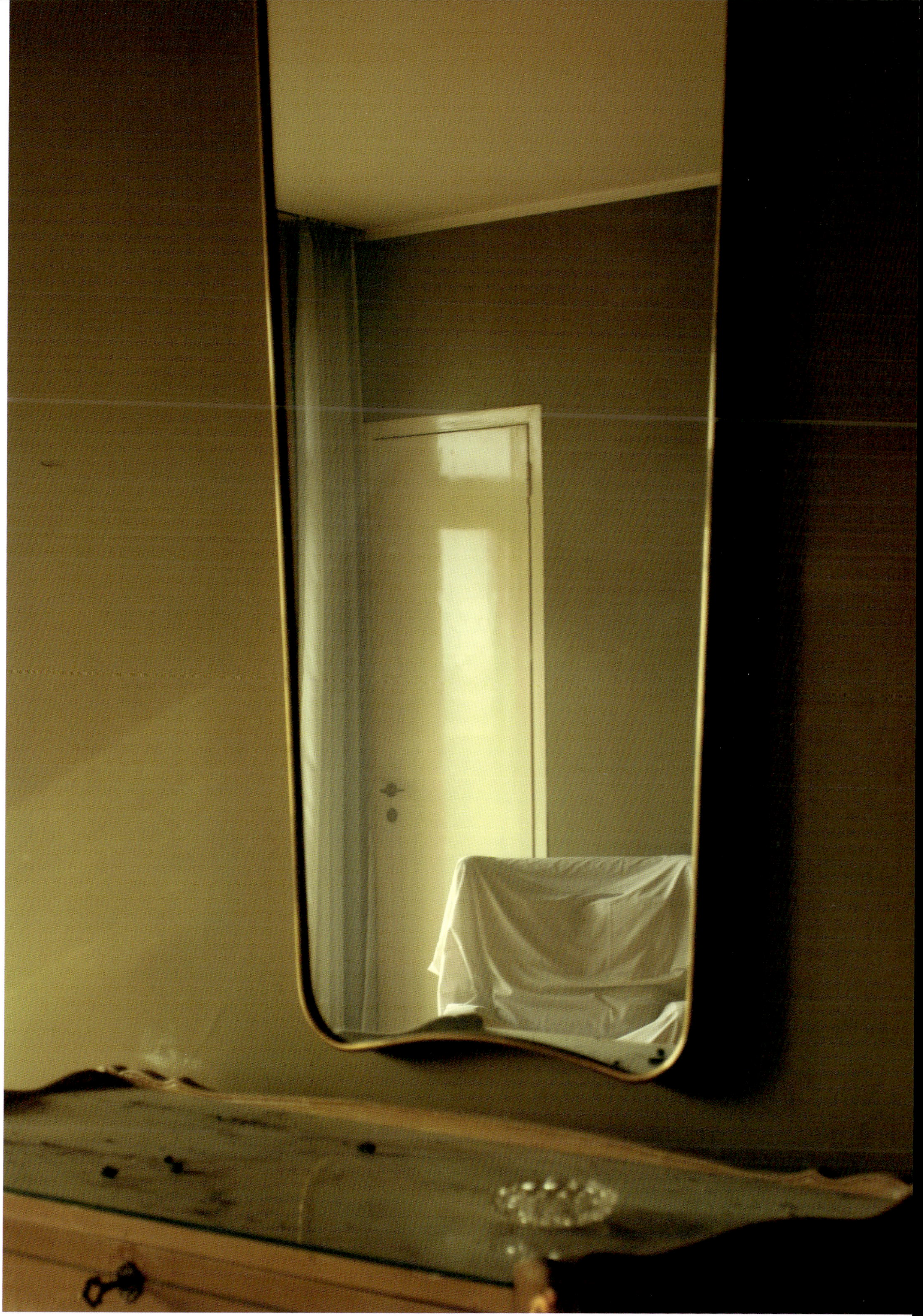

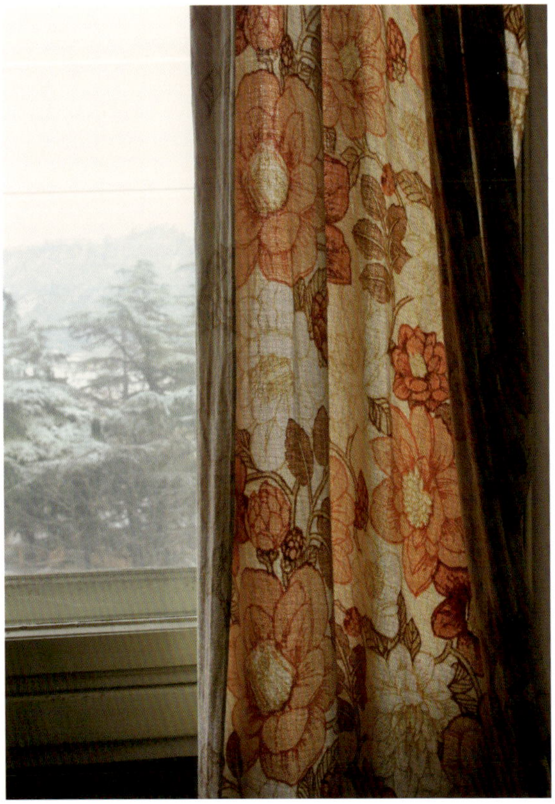

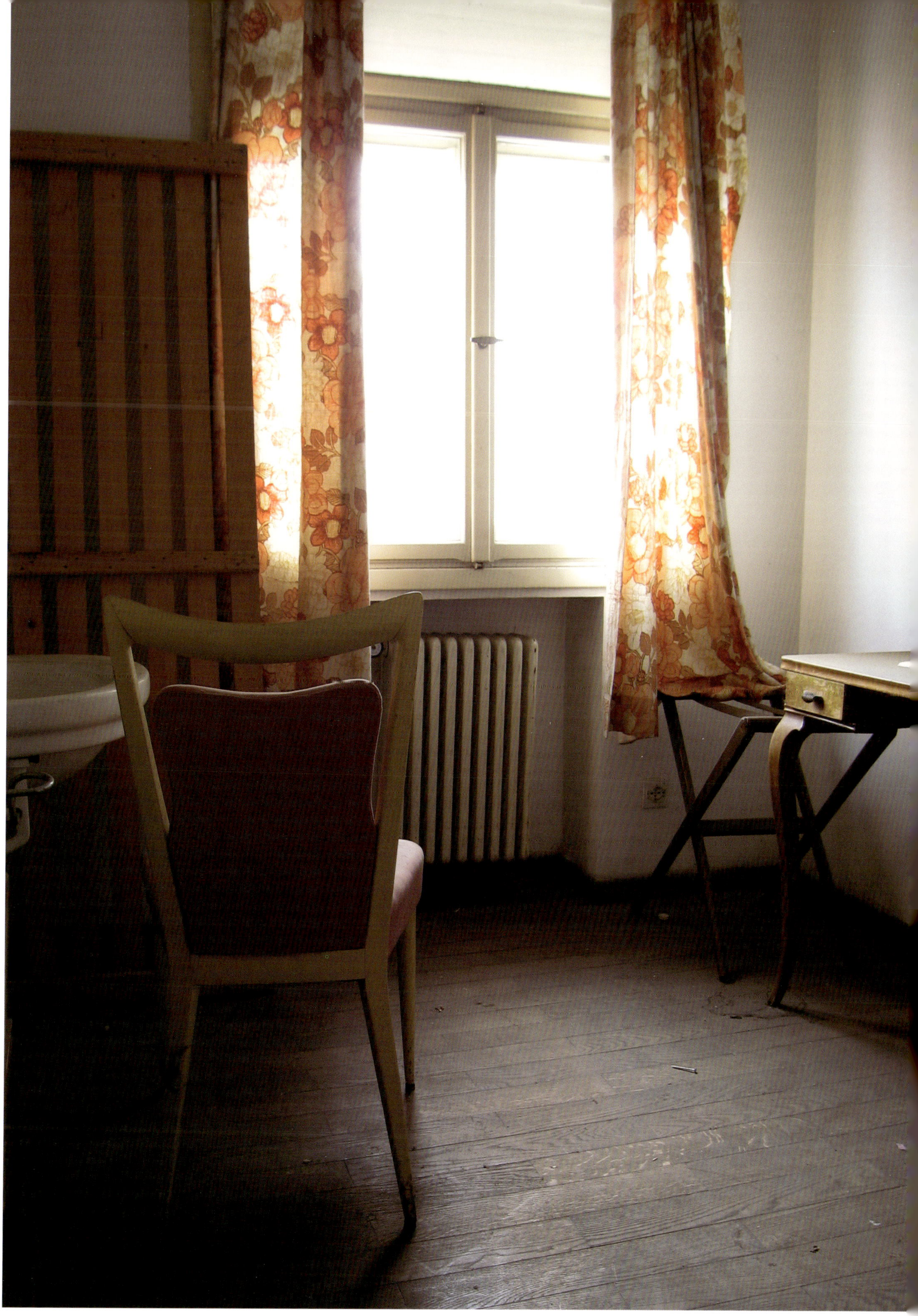

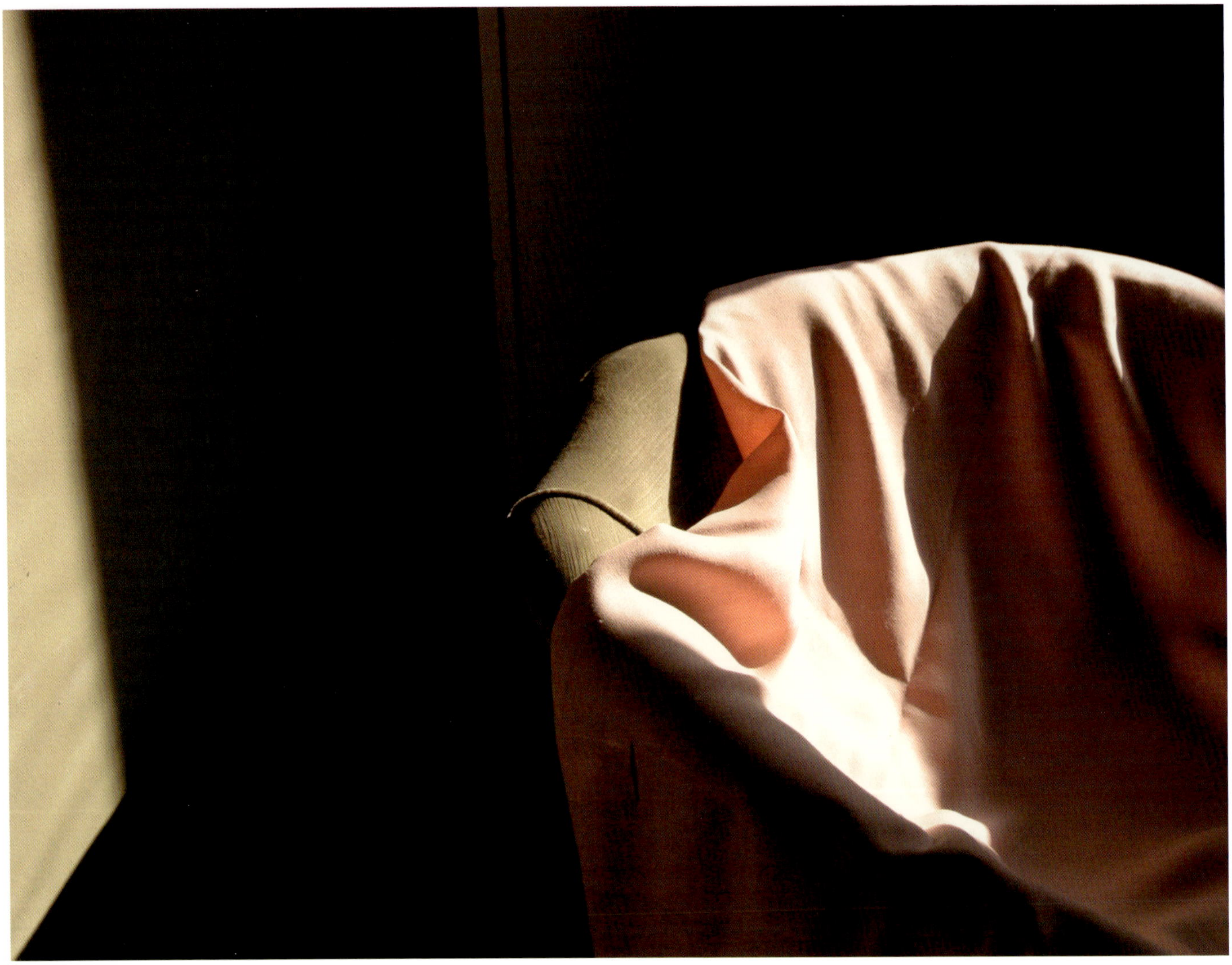

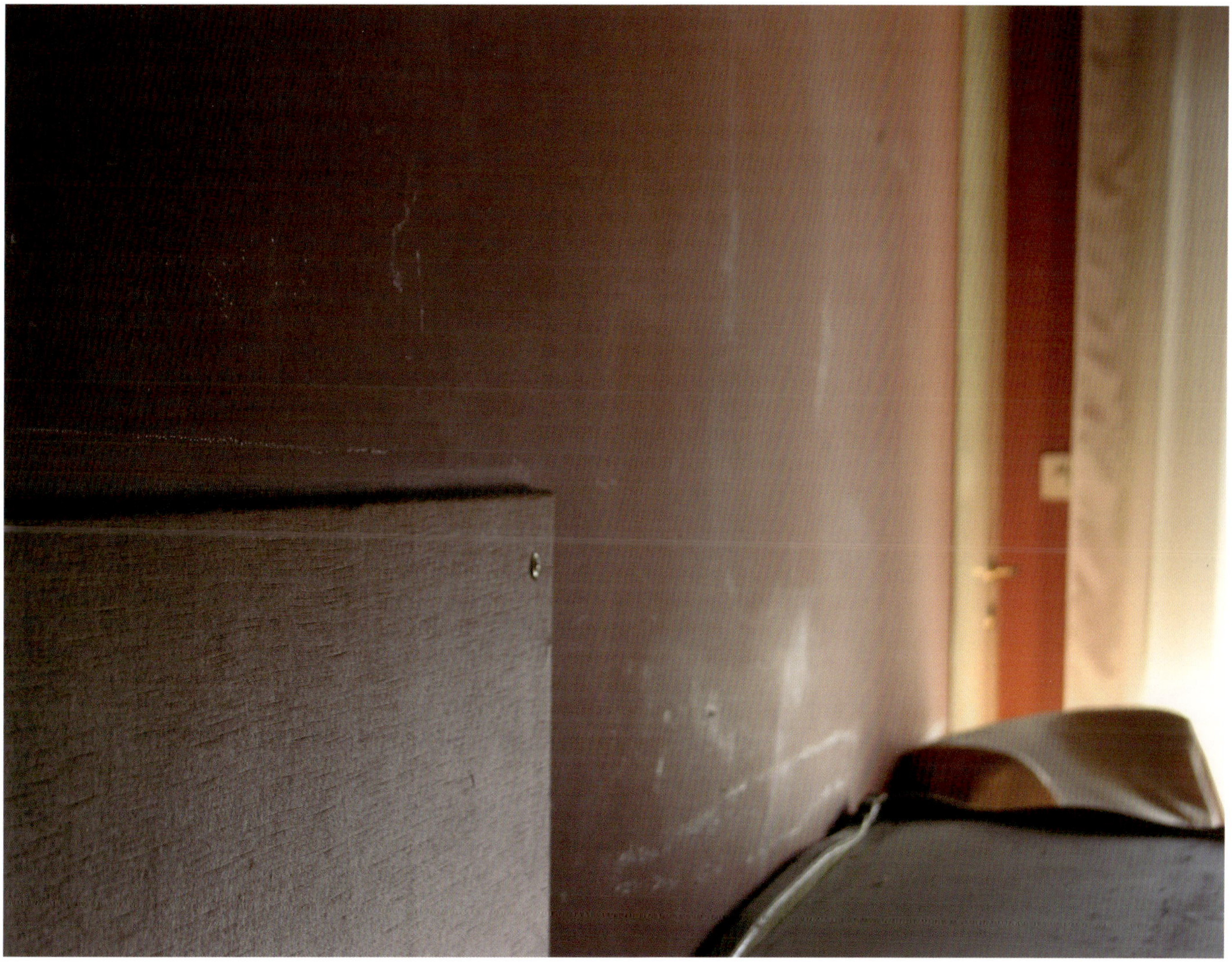

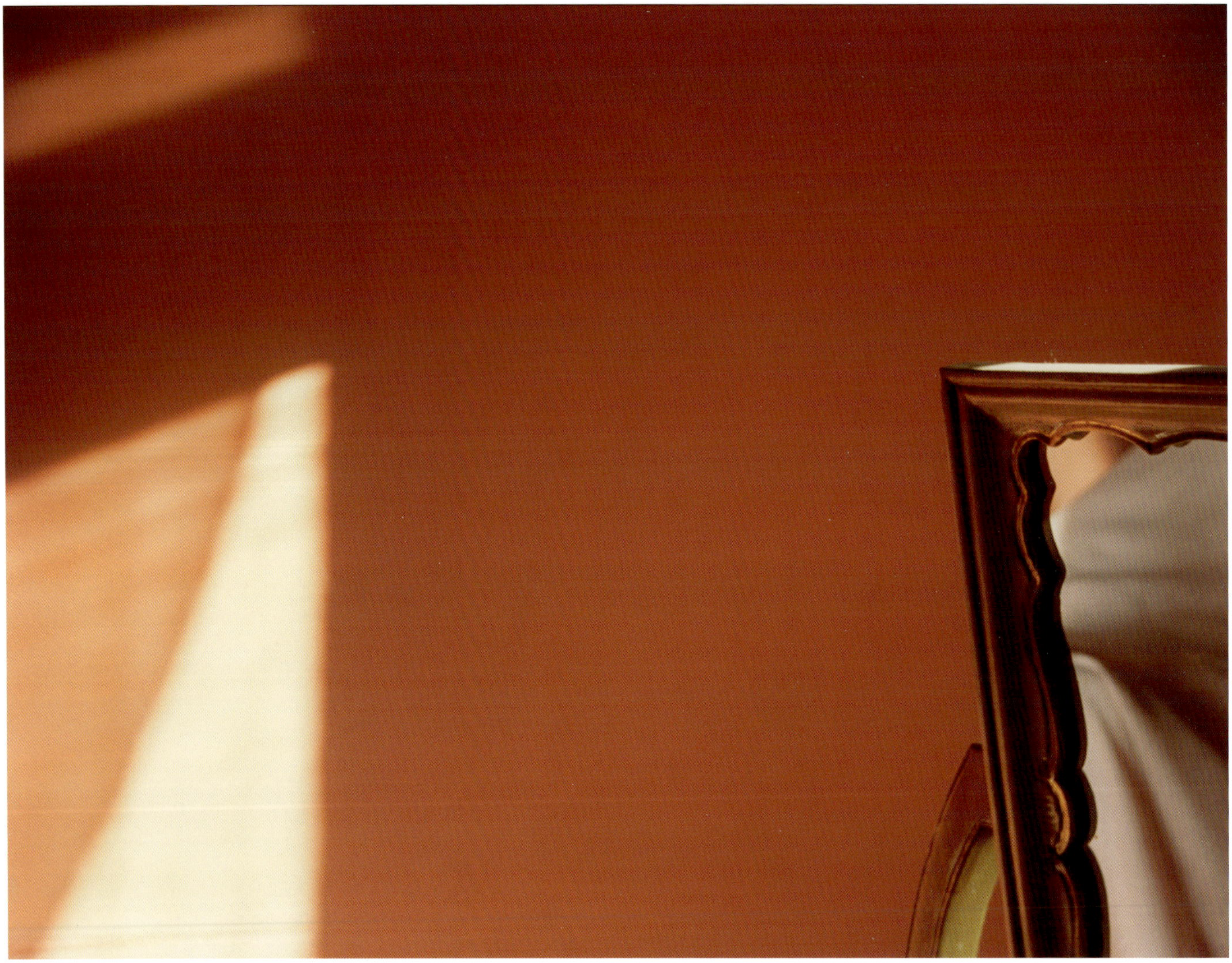

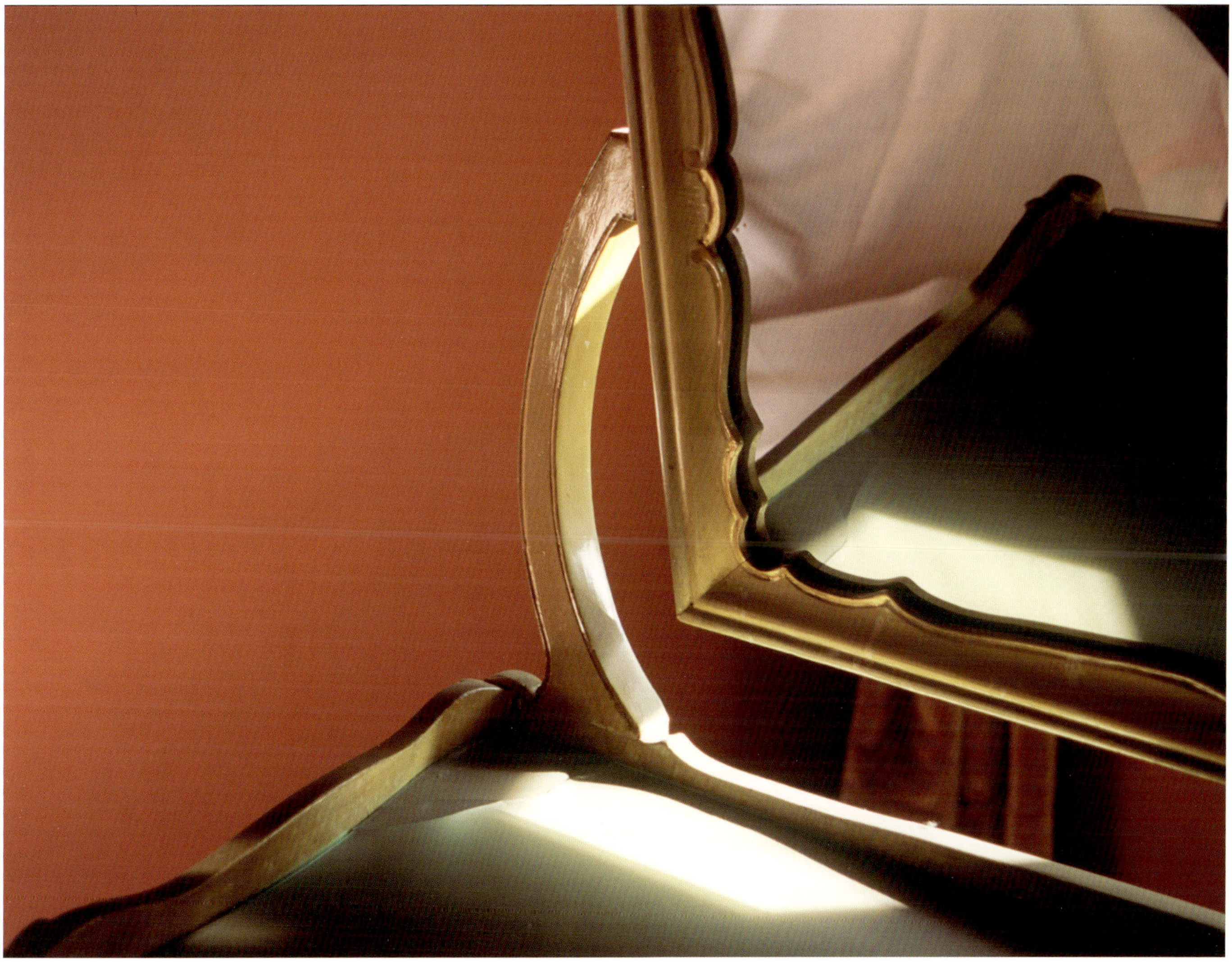

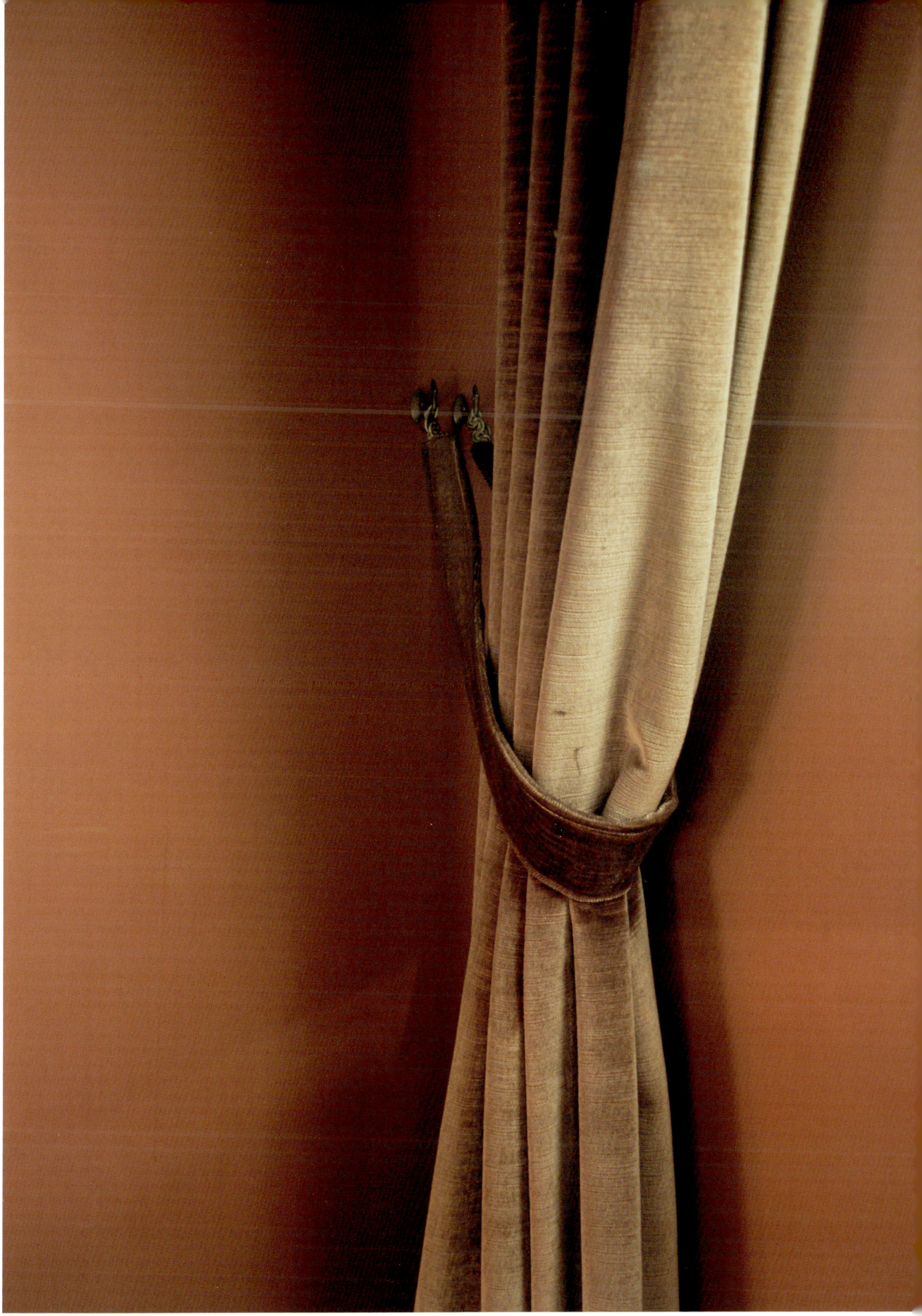

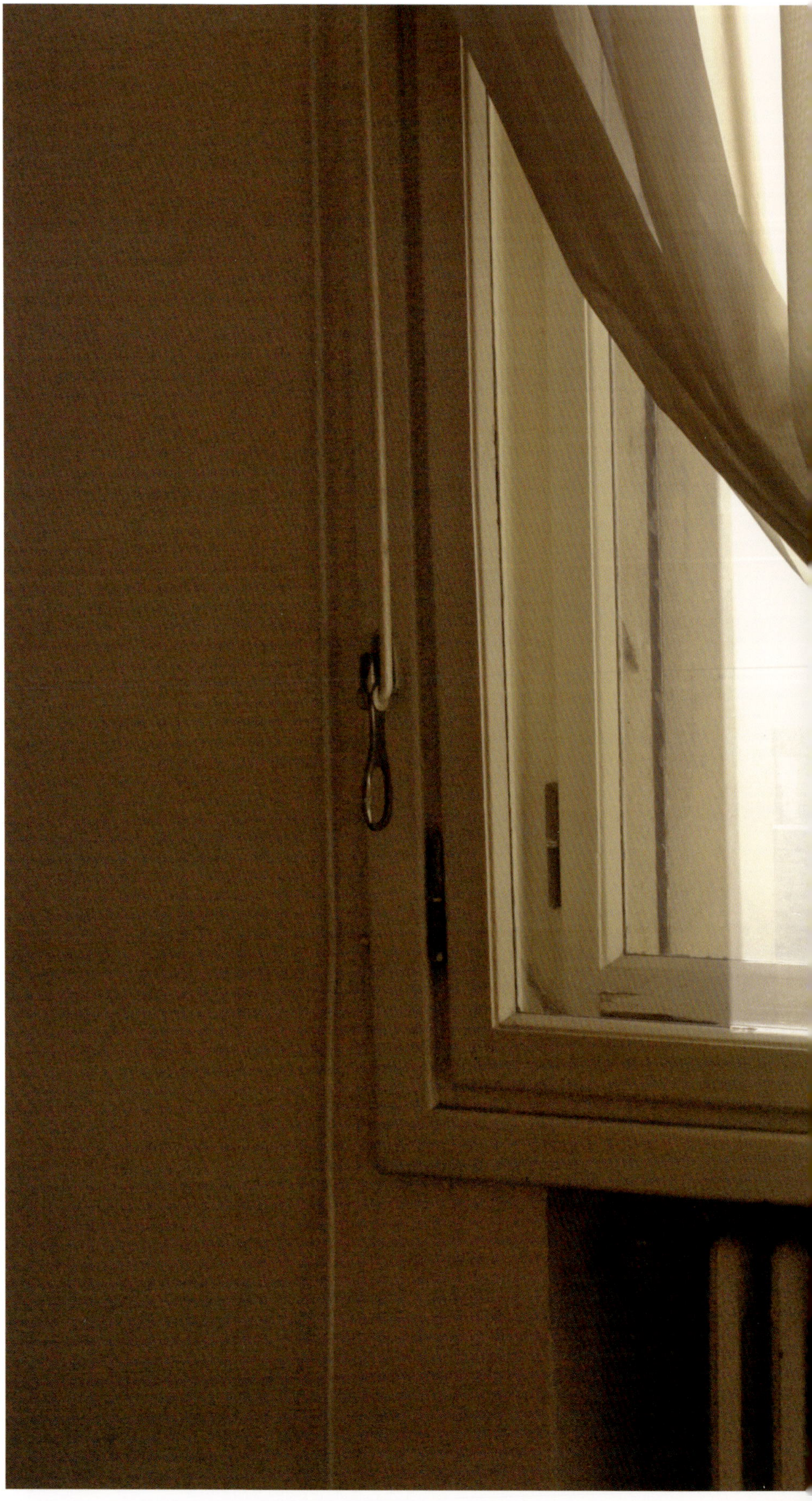

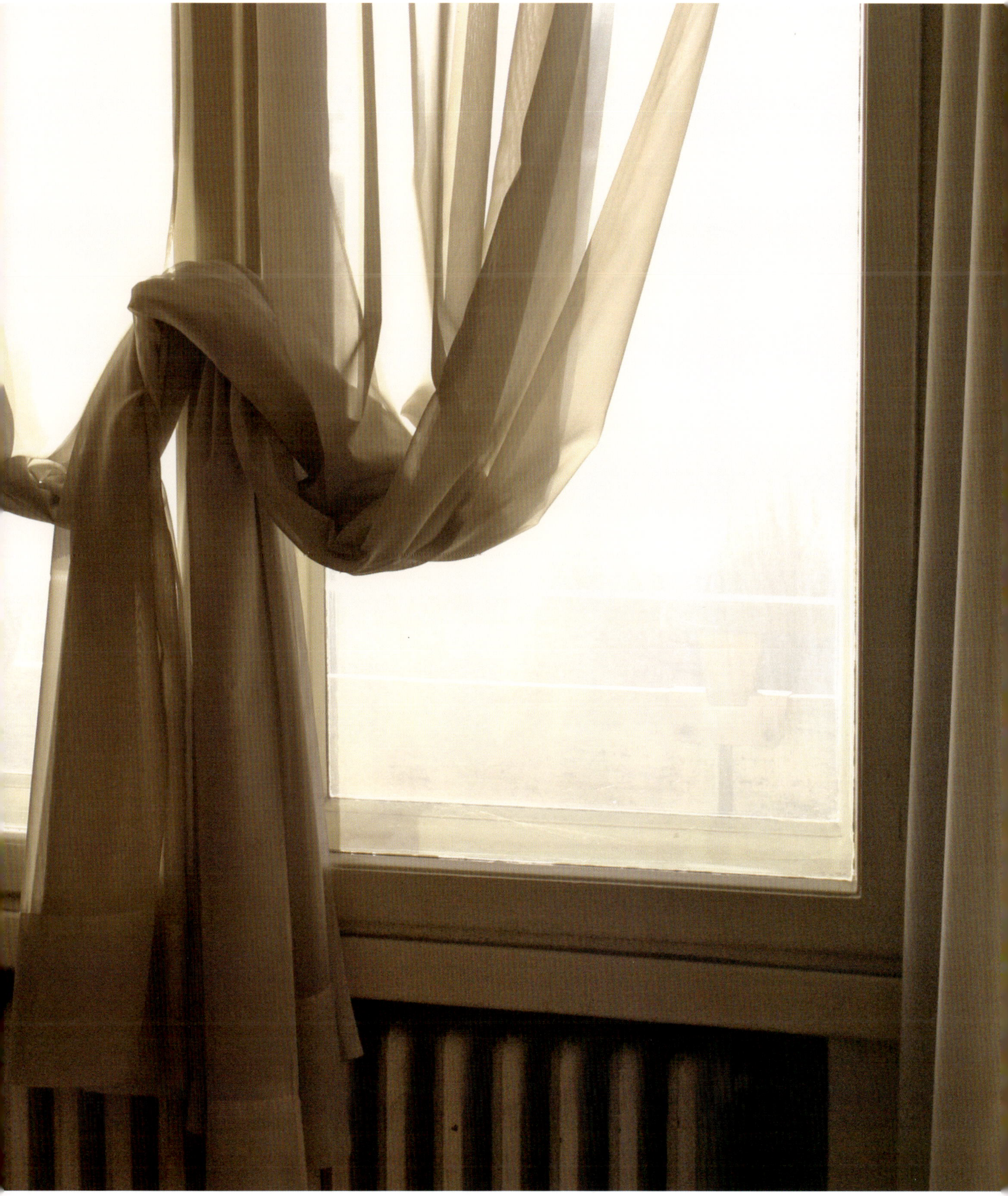

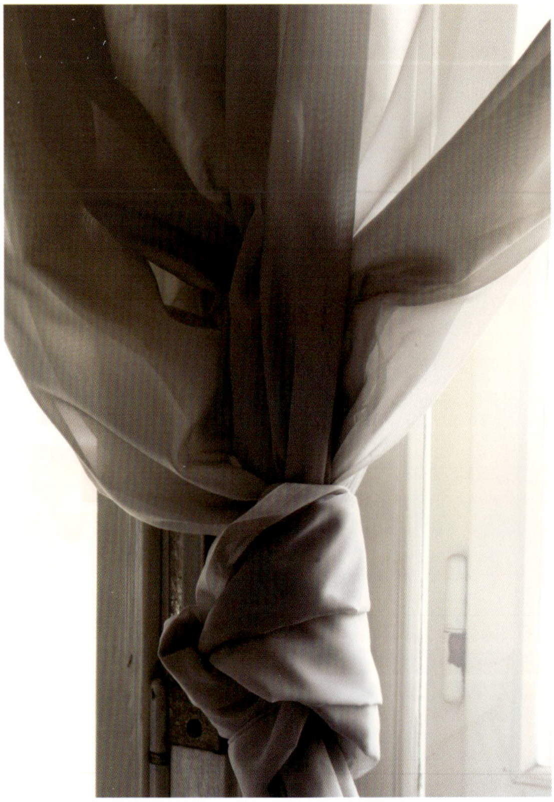

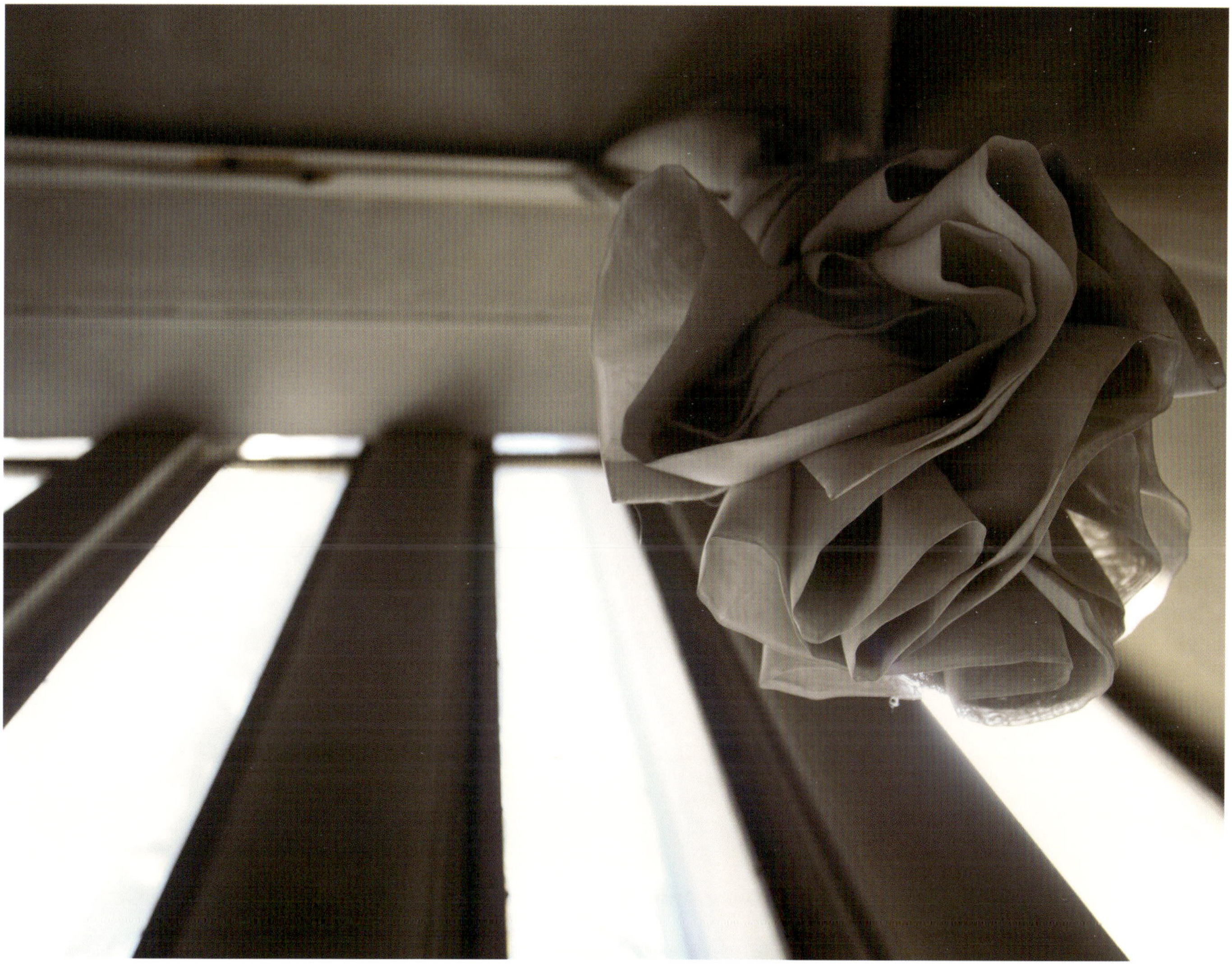

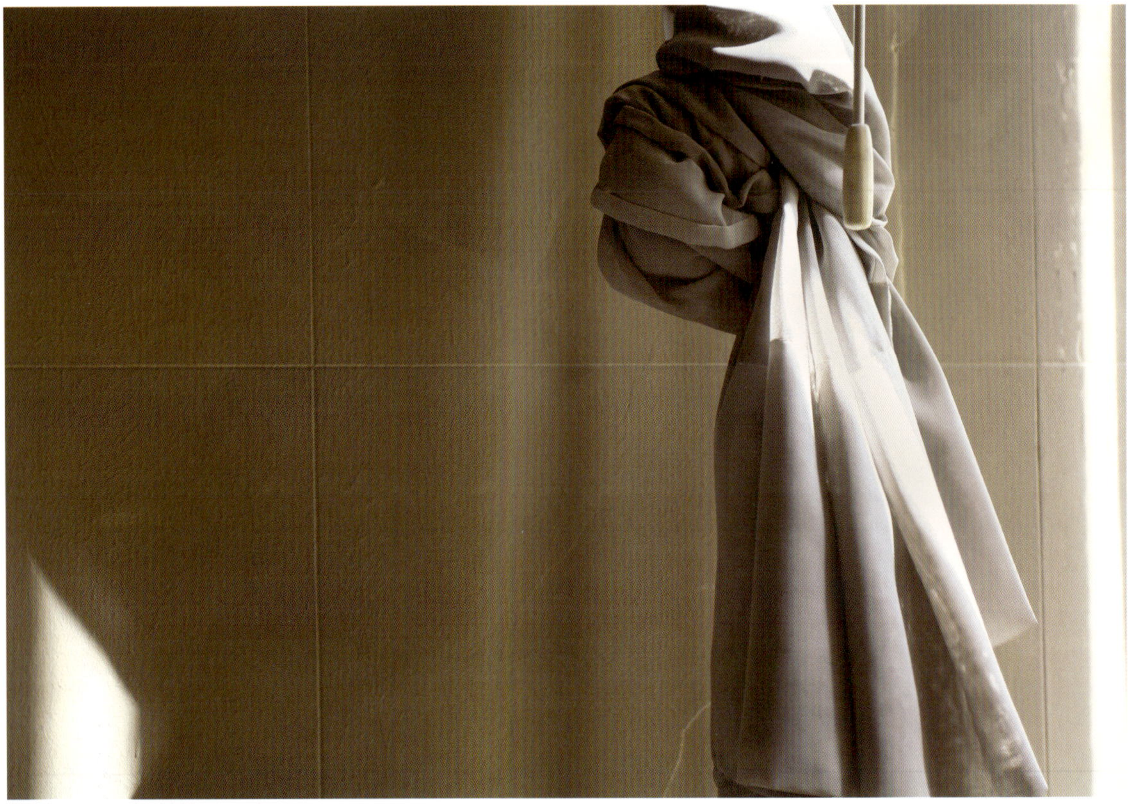

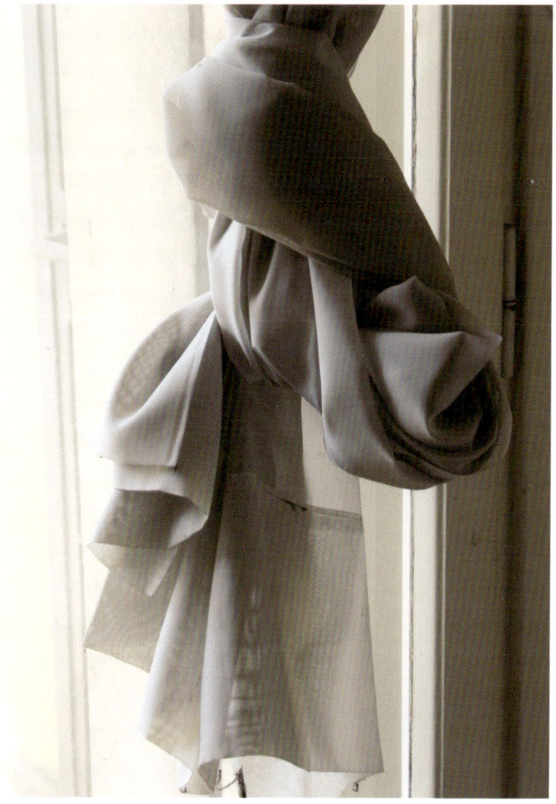

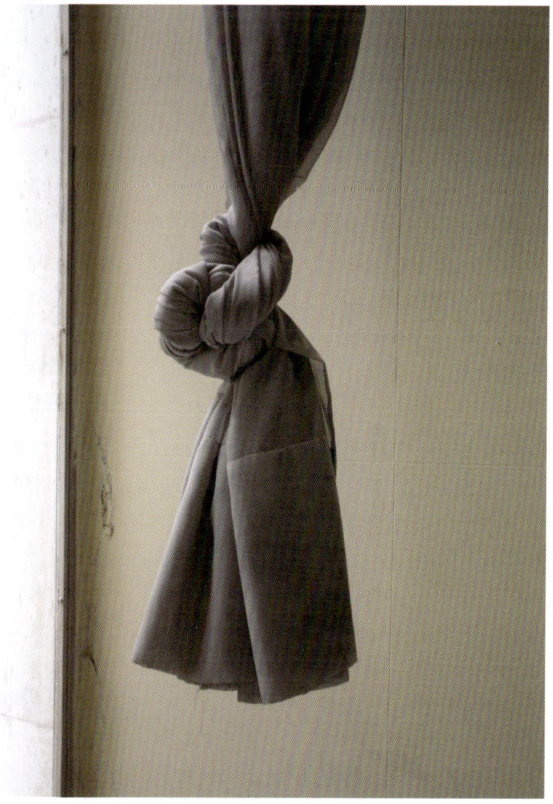

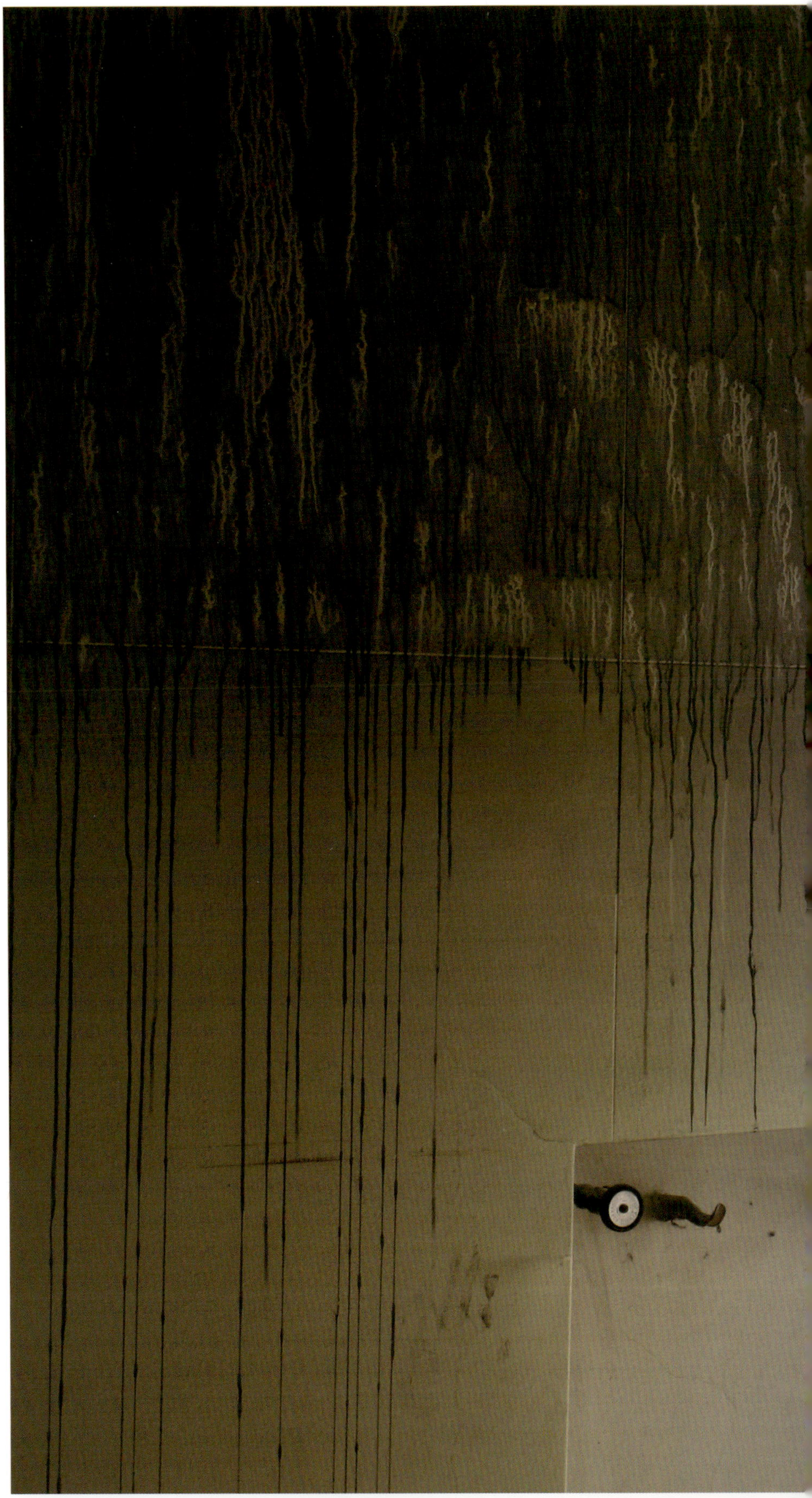

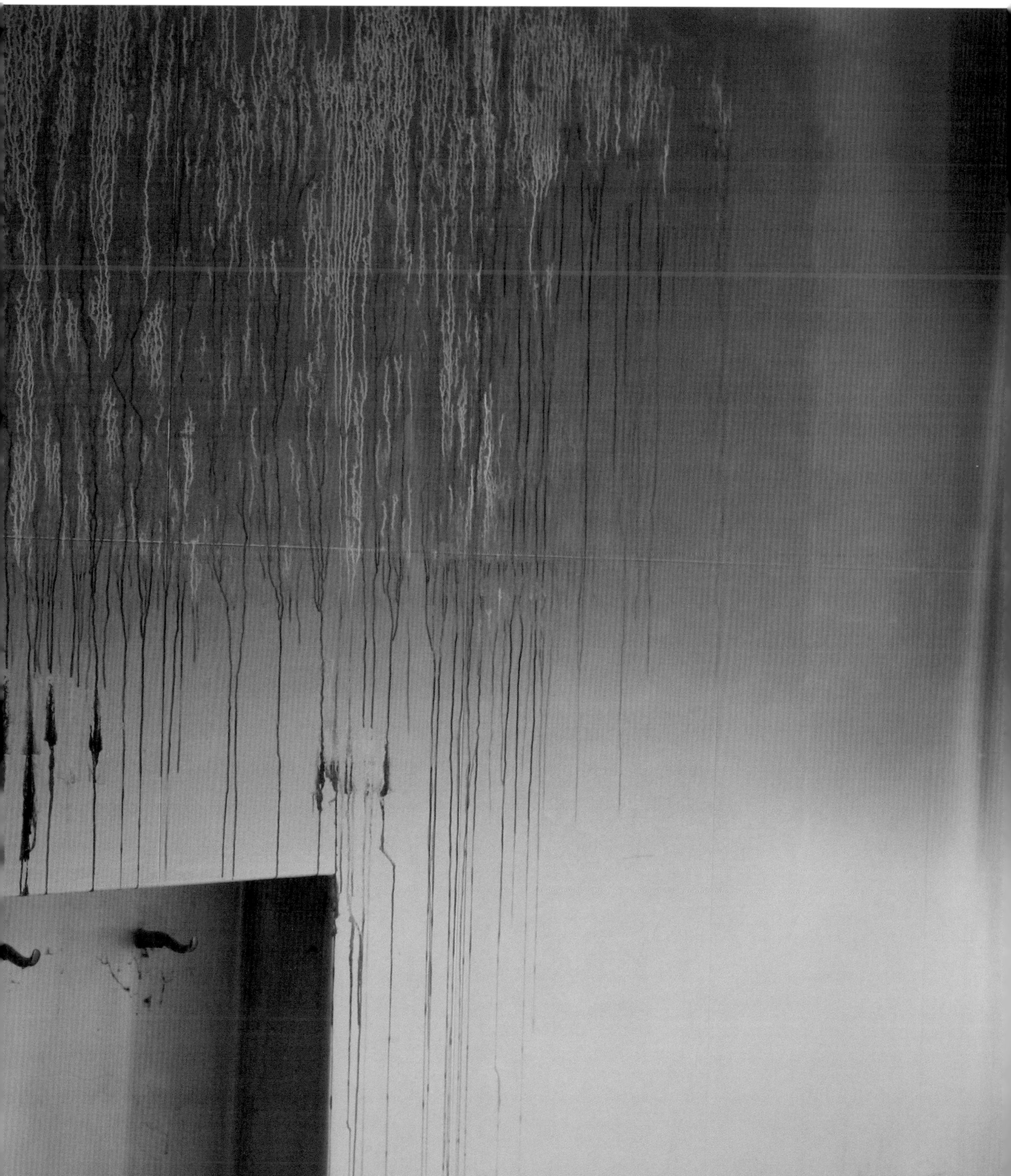

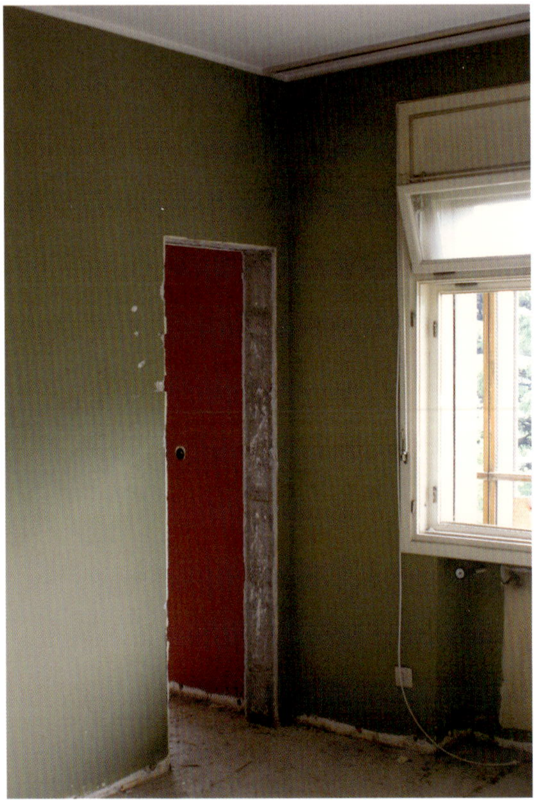

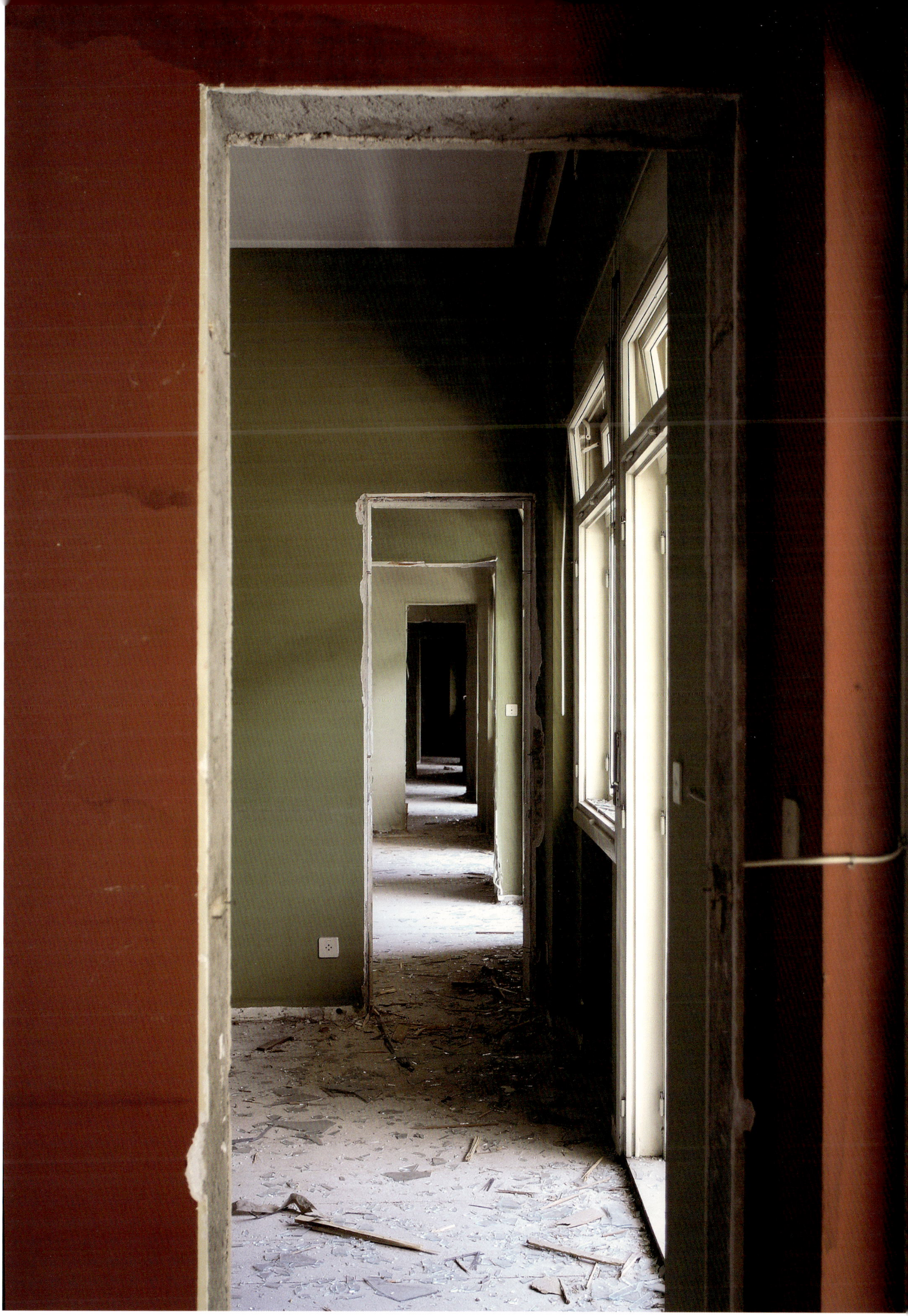

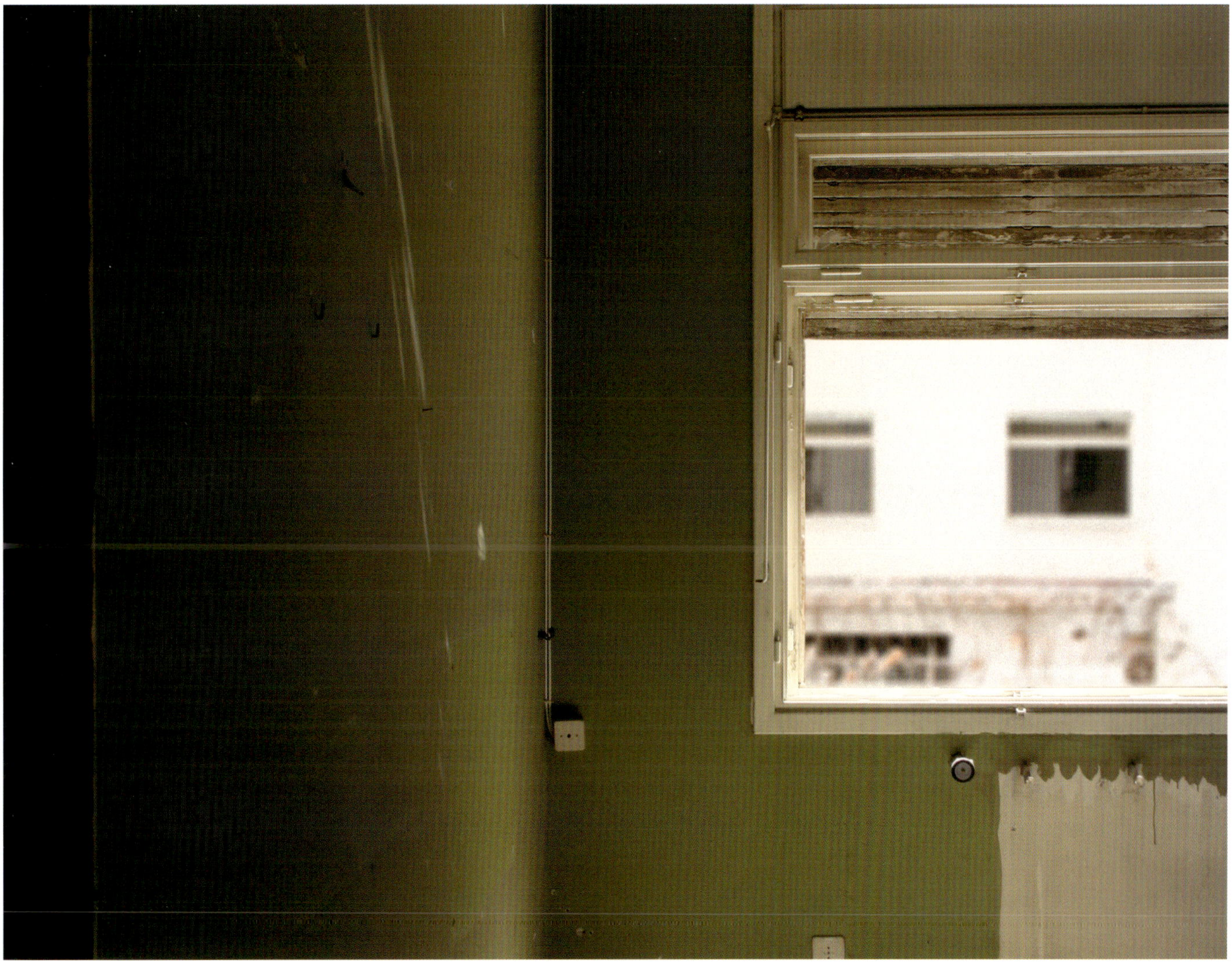

105

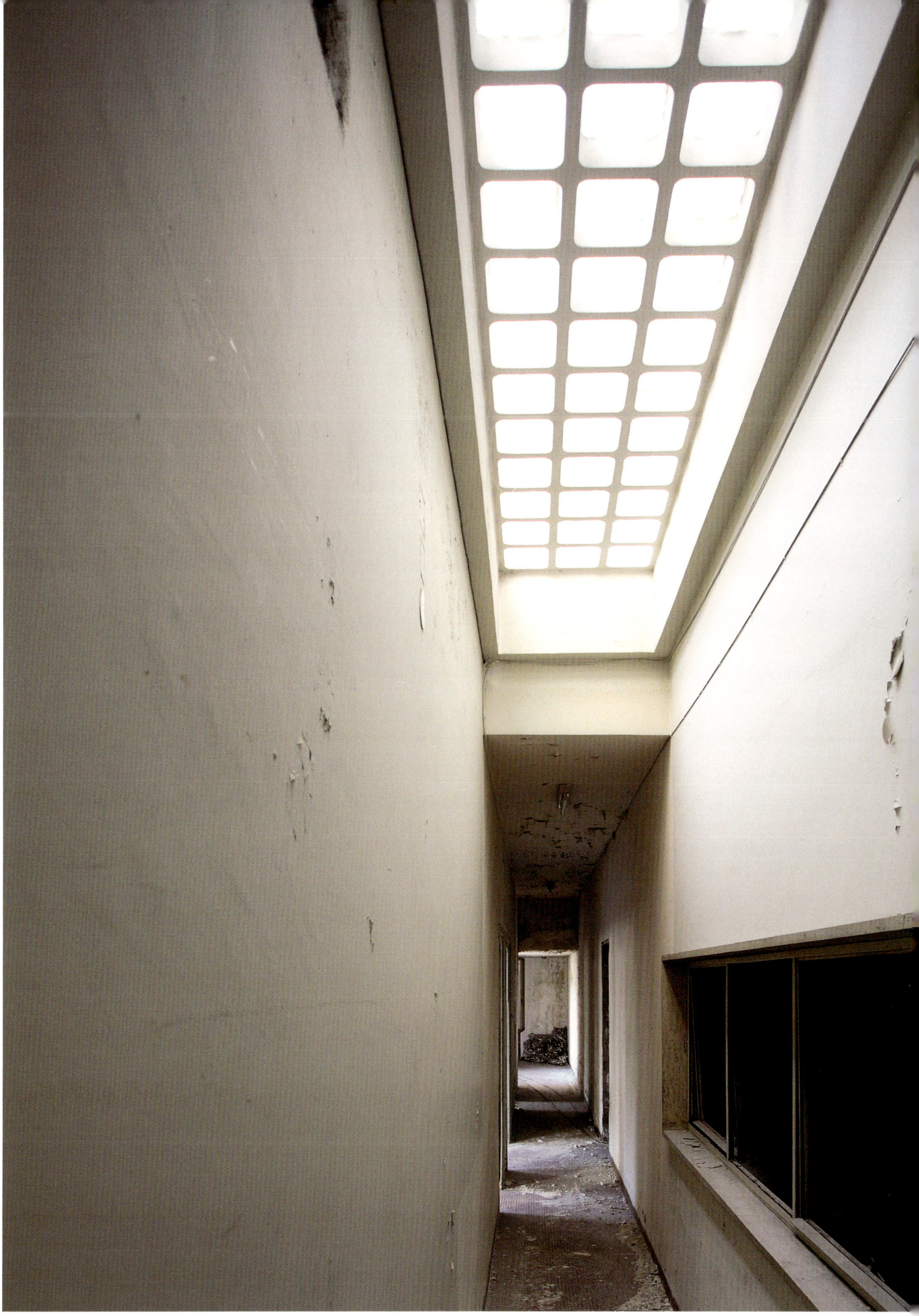

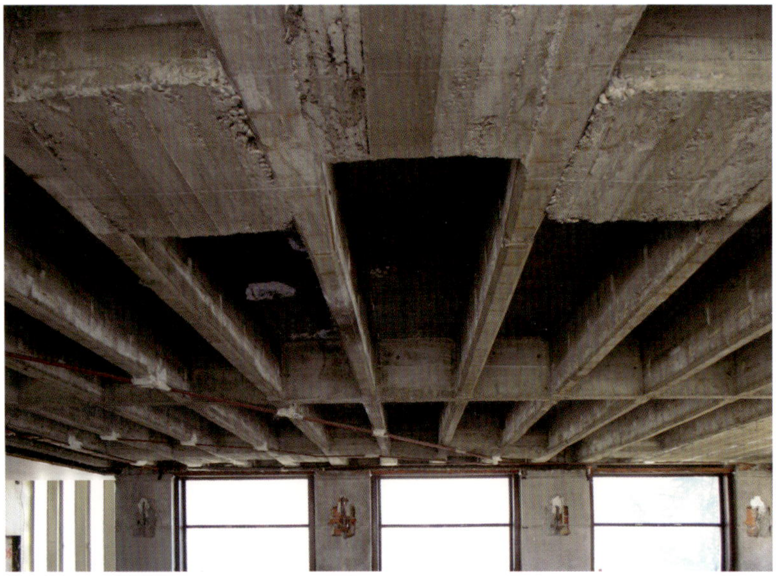

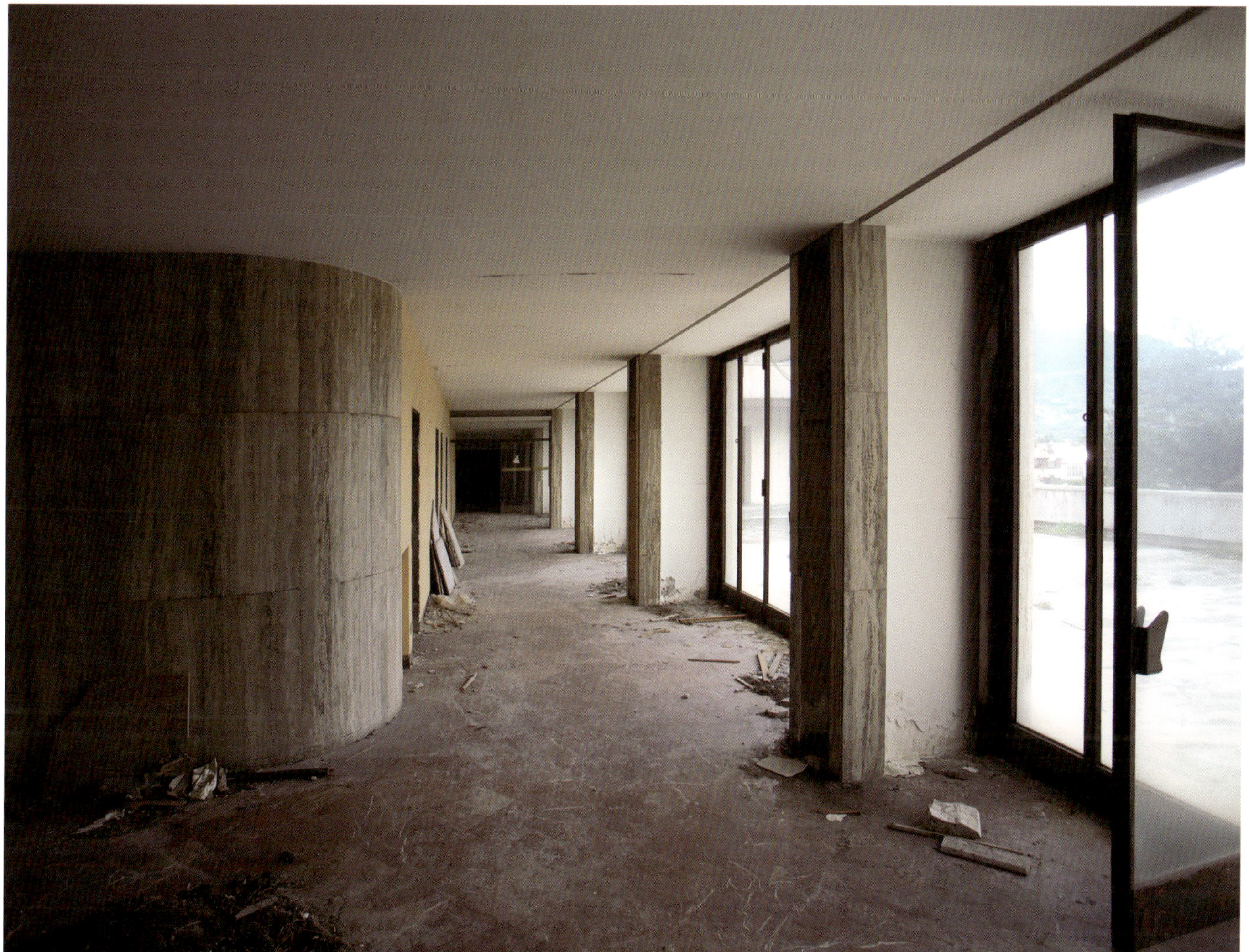

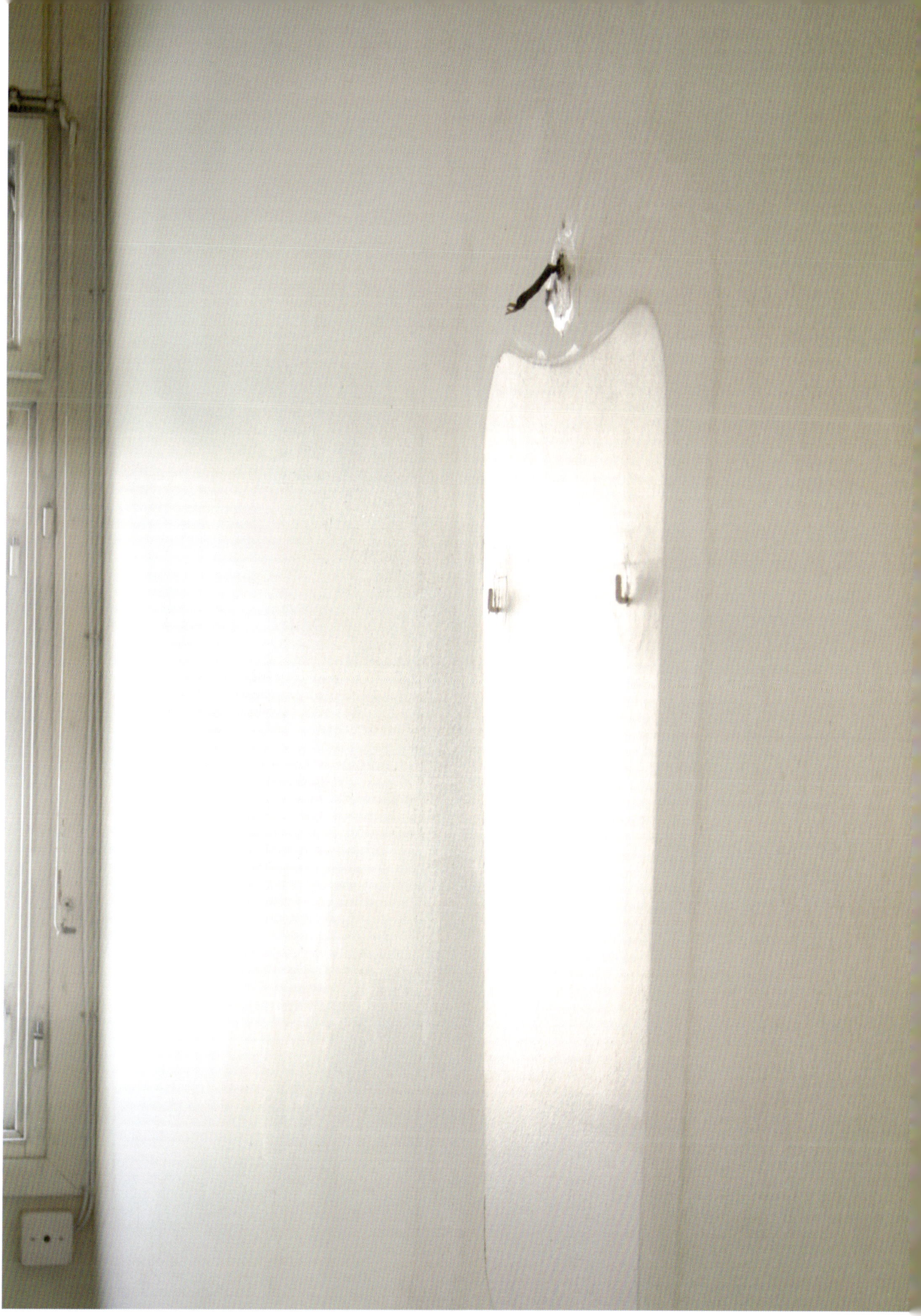

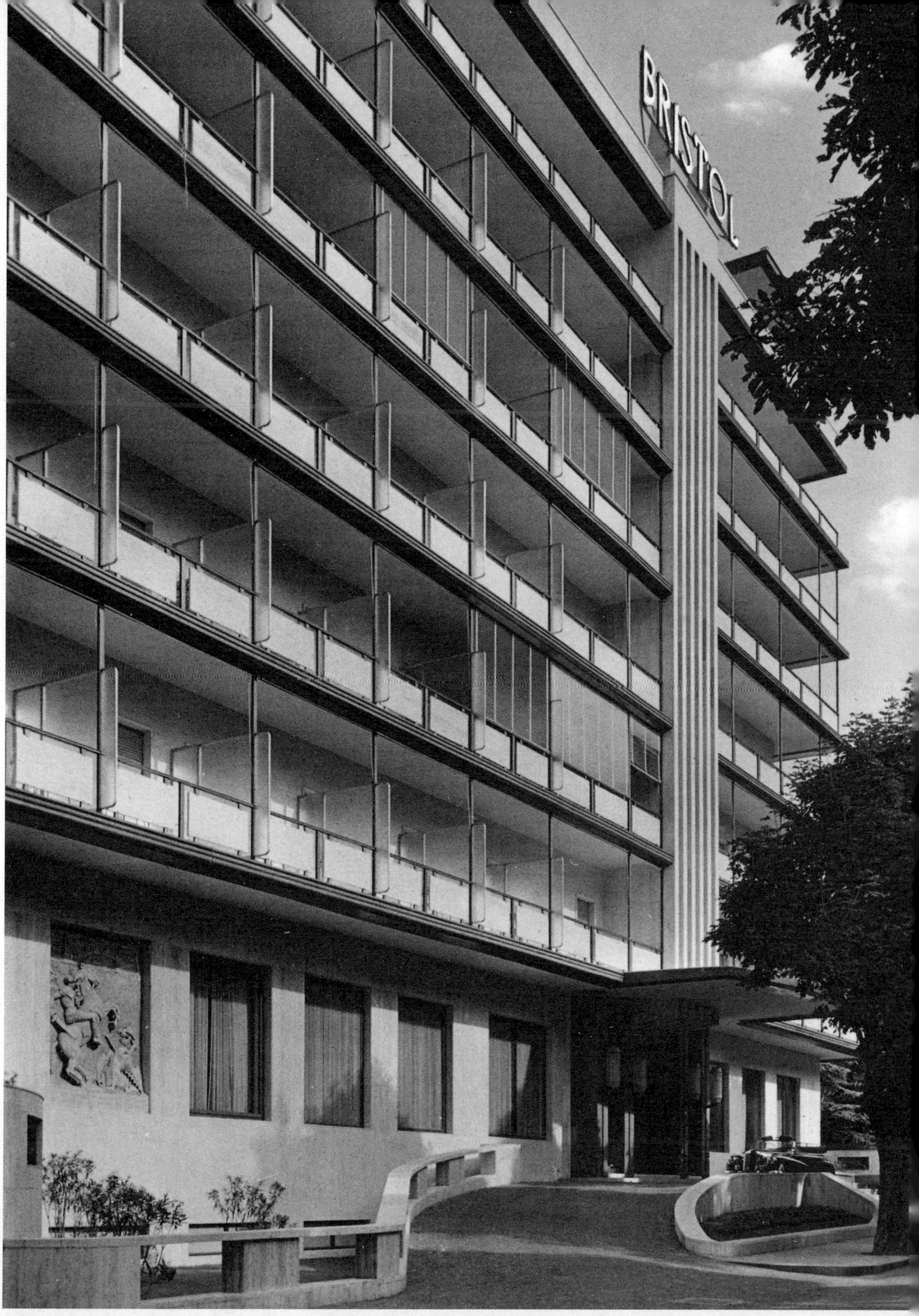
BRISTOL

Hotel Bristol, die Geschichte | Josef Rohrer

Die Teppiche im großen Salon sind längst eingerollt, die Bilder von den mit Seide bespannten Wänden verschwunden, die Lampen aus mundgeblasenem Muranoglas abmontiert. Bagger und Presslufthämmer rücken an und nagen sich durch den riesigen Bau: Durch die Halle, in der die junge Sophia Loren tanzte; durch die Fassade aus weißem Marmor; durch das elegante Treppenhaus bis hinauf zur Dachterrasse mit dem Swimmingpool, den die Weltpresse so bestaunte. Am Ende liegt das Bristol in Meran zu einem riesigen Haufen Schutt und Stahl zerkleinert. Die Reste des Traumes eines schwerreichen Reeders aus Venedig. Mit dem 1954 eröffneten Bristol, das unzählige Zeitungsartikel als das „modernste und eleganteste Hotel Europas" lobten, wollte er aus Meran ein zweites St. Moritz schaffen. Er steckte ungeheure Summen in diesen Traum – und scheiterte.

Diese Erzählung handelt vordergründig von Glanz und Zerfall eines ungewöhnlichen Hotels, das an den falschen Ort gestellt wurde. Dahinter aber kreuzen sich in ihm mehrere spannende Geschichten und verweben sich zu einem Stück Zeitgeschichte. Im Bristol spiegeln sich der Untergang der dekadenten Habsburger-Monarchie, der Größenwahn von Mussolinis Faschismus, das berüchtigte Abkommen von 1939 zwischen Hitler und Mussolini, das kurze Aufflackern des italienischen Nationalstolzes in Südtirol nach dem Zweiten Weltkrieg, der Einfall des Massentourismus, der das Gesicht der Alpen radikal veränderte. Stars und Sternchen, Spieler und Spekulanten, der europäische Geldadel und ein späterer Papst – sie alle tauchen im Bristol auf. Das Hotel ist eine Bühne, auf der im Zeitraffer 100 Jahre Südtirol ablaufen.

Die Geschichte des Bristol beginnt bald nach 1900 mit einem gleichnamigen Vorgängerbau. In der angeblichen Belle Époque erlebt das südliche Tirol eine kurze Glanzzeit. Das einst rückständige Bauernland überholt das bis dahin führende Böhmen und steigt zur beliebtesten Ferienregion Österreich-Ungarns auf. Der „Südbalkon der Monarchie" boomt, Meran quillt über. Der Hochadel sowie neureiches Publikum aus Deutschland, Russland und den österreichischen Kronländern flanieren über die Promenaden, zahlreiche Hotels entstehen. Das Potenzial scheint unbegrenzt und lockt immer neue Investoren an. Und so baut 1908 eine deutsche Fabrikantenfamilie an der heutigen Freiheitsstraße ein weiteres Großhotel im Stil der Zeit. Das erste Bristol zeigt stolz sein neoklassizistisches Outfit mit Giebeln und Säulen, überbordendem Stuck und opulenten Gesellschaftsräumen. Sechs Jahre später bricht der Erste Weltkrieg aus. Wie fast alle anderen größeren Hotels in Meran verwandelt sich auch das Bristol über Nacht in ein Lazarett.

Auf das Kriegsende folgt die Trennung von Österreich, aus dem Südbalkon der Monarchie wird die nördlichste Provinz Italiens. Italiener, die im Tiroler Tourismus der Jahrhundertwende noch keine Rolle spielten, nehmen ihre neue Provinz nun auch reisend in Besitz. Mit den ersten Touristen trifft 1921 eine dramatische Nachricht für das Bristol ein. Italien hat auf seinem Gebiet die Immobilien deutscher Staatsbürger als Ersatz für erlittene Kriegsschäden konfisziert. Ohne diese Enteignung wäre die Geschichte des Bristol so verlaufen wie die vieler anderer Hotels. So aber nimmt sie einen eigenen Weg. Das Bristol wird wie die meisten der enteigneten Besitzungen der „Opera Nazionale per i Combattenti" (ONC) übertragen, einem Hilfsfonds für ehemalige italienische Frontkämpfer, der nach der „Niederlage von Karfreit" zur Hebung der Kampfmoral gegründet worden war. Zunächst will die ONC das Hotel zu Geld machen. Als sich kein Käufer findet, beschließt der nunmehr unter Mussolini stehende Staatsapparat, es für seine Italianisierungspolitik einzusetzen.

Das Bristol ist ein Steinchen in einem Mosaik, in dem die weitgehend von Deutschsprachigen dominierte Tourismuswirtschaft Südtirols eine Tricolore-Färbung erhalten soll. Um 1930 plant der Mailänder Stararchitekt Paolo Vietti-Violi in Meran einen riesigen Pferderennplatz. Mussolini kümmert sich persönlich um das Projekt. 1936 wird es mit dem „Gran Premio di Merano" eingeweiht. Das schwere Flachrennen ist seitdem eines der Highlights im italienischen Pferdesport. Als 1932 nicht weit von Meran Quellen mit leicht radioaktivem Wasser entdeckt werden, plant Vietti-Violi auch eine Thermenanlage, die zu der Zeit die größte Europas geworden wäre. Gebaut wird sie allerdings nie. Ein weiterer Mailänder Architekt hat ebenfalls Großes vor. Gio Ponti, der später durch das Pirelli-Hochhaus in Mailand berühmt wird, entwirft eine gigantische Skischaukel, die sich zwischen Bozen, Gröden und Cortina über die gesamten Dolomiten spannen soll: 150 Kilometer Seilbahn, unterbrochen von luxuriösen Mittelstationen, die Hotelanlage, Einkaufszentrum und Vergnügungspark in einem sein sollen. Auch dieser große Wurf bleibt eine Skizze auf dem Papier. Von seinen geplanten Hotelanlagen baut Ponti nur einen für seine Architektur vielfach gelobten Prototypen, das „Paradiso del Cevedale" in der Ortlergruppe. Seine Geschichte wird sich später mit der des neuen Bristol kreuzen.

Dem alten Bristol bekommt die Geschäftsführung der ONC nicht. Mitte der 1930er Jahre ist der Glanz des Jahrhundertwende-Hotels weitgehend verblasst. Als dann auch noch das Optionsabkommen zwischen Hitler und Mussolini umzusetzen ist, muss die ONC aus Staatsräson im Bristol für die „Amtliche Deutsche Ein- und Rückwanderungs-Stelle" Platz schaffen. Diese Behörde soll ab 1939 die von Hitler und Mussolini beschlossene Umsiedlung der deutsch- und ladinischsprachigen Südtiroler in ein neues Gebiet des Deutschen Reichs organisieren. Mit dem Einmarsch der deutschen Wehrmacht in Italien ist das sogenannte Optionsabkommen jedoch Makulatur. Ins Bristol ziehen nun deutsche Heeresstellen ein. Als der Krieg endlich aus ist, ist es als Hotel kaum noch zu gebrauchen. Wie Phönix aus der Asche wächst aus dem alten jedoch ein neues Bristol. Ende der 1940er Jahre kommt der venezianische Reeder Arnaldo Bennati zufällig nach Meran. Weil einer seiner Söhne herzkrank ist und an schwerem Asthma leidet, begleitet er ihn zur Kur und verliebt sich in die Stadt. Der gebürtige Genueser ist nach dem Krieg einer der reichsten Männer Norditaliens. Er besitzt neben seiner florierenden Reederei mit dem Bauer-Grünwald auch eines der besten Hotels von Venedig. In Meran ist Bennati von den Möglichkeiten angetan, die sich ihm dort zu bieten scheinen. 1950 kauft er das Bristol, in einer Zeit, in der der Tourismus darnieder liegt und etliche der Meraner Großhotels geschlossen bleiben. Die ONC ist heilfroh, diese Immobilie endlich los zu sein. Bennati denkt zunächst daran, den Bau zu sanieren und um einen Seitenflügel zu erweitern. Dann aber lässt er das alte Bristol kurzerhand niederreißen; einen amtlichen Denkmalschutz gibt es noch nicht. Ein neues, größeres Bristol muss an seiner Stelle her, etwas, worüber die ganze Welt staunen soll.

Und sie staunt. Das neue Bristol plant der venezianische Schiffsarchitekt Marino Meo. Der erste Entwurf ist ein Würfel mit Innenhof. Als er schon zwei Stockwerke hoch gebaut ist, lässt Bennati Teile davon wieder niederreißen. Das Konzept, welches das Schwimmbad noch im Garten vor dem Hotel vorsah, ist ihm nicht spektakulär genug. Erst mit dem zweiten Entwurf ist er zufrieden. Das Gebäude hat nun die Form eines H, und das Schwimmbad mit seinem drei Meter tiefen Becken liegt auf der Dachterrasse im sechsten Stock. Das hat die Welt noch nicht gesehen. Als das neue Bristol nach über zweijähriger Bauzeit fertig ist, hat es den ungeheuren Betrag von 1,5 Milliarden Lire gekostet. Für dieses Geld bekäme man zu der Zeit in Florenz zwei der größten Hotels. Das Bristol ist voll klimatisiert – ein Luxus, den sich zu jener Zeit nicht einmal das Waldorf-Astoria in New York leistet. Alle 137 Zimmer und 20 Luxussuiten haben TV-Anschluss, obwohl das Fernsehen erst zwei Jahre später in die Region kommt. Und aus Persien hat Bennati eine ganze Schiffsladung Teppiche kommen lassen, angeblich über 1000 Stück. Im spektakulären Salon mit den Wänden aus Onyx liegen sie sechs Zentimeter hoch. Im Luster darüber brennen 1000 Glühbirnen zwischen 1500 mundgeblasenen Plättchen aus Muranoglas. Für seinen Spleen war dem Reeder nichts zu teuer.

Stargast der Eröffnungsfeier im Sommer 1954 ist die 20-jährige Sophia Loren, der neue Stern am Kinohimmel. Und die Segnung des neuen Bristol überlässt Bennati dem Patriarchen von Venedig, Angelo Giuseppe Roncalli, der wenig später als Papst Johannes XXIII. berühmt wird. Während die meisten Südtiroler im neuen Hotel nur den „walschen Kasten" sehen, der ihnen stets fremd bleiben wird, lobt die italienische und internationale Presse in unzähligen Artikeln das Bristol als eines der „modernsten und elegantesten Hotels Europas". Selbst die New York Times widmet dem „auffallend modernen Bristol" einen großen Beitrag. 360 Artikel erscheinen in den ersten Monaten über das neue Hotel, seine Architektur und das Interieur gelten als Sensation. In den besseren Zimmern stehen venezianische Faschingsfiguren als Lampen, in den Wandleuchten aus Muranoglas ist Goldstaub eingesprenkelt, überall findet sich Marmor und Edelholz, viele Wände sind mit Tapeten aus Seide verkleidet. Und spätestens am Pool auf dem Dach wähnt man sich an Bord eines Luxusliners, der in den Bergen vor Anker liegt. So viel Glamour ist ein Magnet für die High Society. Italiens Oberschicht steigt nun im Bristol ab. Die Pirellis kommen, die Lebensmittelfabrikanten Invernizzi, aber auch die Flicks aus Deutschland. Meran scheint an seine guten Zeiten an der Jahrhundertwende anzuknüpfen, als der europäische Hoch- und Geldadel zur Kur angereist war. Der italienische Automobilclub hält nun im Bristol seine Jahreskongresse ab, begleitet von Auftritten der Sophia Loren. Mike Bongiorno, der Star des jungen italienischen Fernsehens, moderiert dort eine Show, auf der Dachterrasse trifft man sich zu Modeschauen, und selbstverständlich finden die um den Großen Preis von Meran inszenierten Galaabende nun im Bristol statt. Immer wieder ist das Hotel auch Kulisse für Filmaufnahmen. Wie 1957 für „Mein Schatz ist aus Tirol" mit den Kessler-Zwillingen und Joachim Fuchsberger. In diesem deutschen Heimatfilm treten Meraner als Statisten auf – eine der wenigen Gelegenheiten, zu denen die Einheimischen ins Bristol dürfen. Denn dort passen Kellner oder Köche aus Tirol nicht ins Bild. Das Personal soll dem mondänen Flair entsprechen und kommt von auswärts.

Arnaldo Bennati will jedoch mehr als nur ein außergewöhnliches Hotel. Bald nach der Eröffnung des Bristol kauft er im Martelltal das 1936 von Gio Ponti gebaute „Paradiso del Cevedale". Ohne Respekt vor diesem herausragenden Beispiel moderner Hotelarchitektur lässt er ein Stockwerk aufsetzen, einen Flügel anbauen und das dezente Olivgrün mit einem kräftigen venezianischen Rot übertünchen. Das „Paradiso" auf 2000 Meter Meereshöhe schwebt ihm als extravagante Dependance des Bristol in Meran und des Bauer-Grünwald in Venedig vor, erreichbar nicht nur über eine neue Straße, sondern auch mit einem Hubschrauber-Shuttle, der vom Dach des Bristol starten soll. Die phantastischen Projekte Bennatis werden von einer Seilbahn abgerundet, die vom Bristol auf die Mut, einen der Meraner Hausberge, führen soll. Hinter all dem soll sich das Glücksspiel drehen, in dem Bennati den Antrieb für seine schöne, neue Tourismuswelt sieht. In Meran war schon mehrfach versucht worden, ein Casino zu etablieren. Jeweils vor und nach den beiden Weltkriegen wurde im Kurhaus gezockt und gepokert, doch nur im diffusen Licht an der Grenze zur Legalität. 1947 wird das Glücksspiel offiziell verboten. Der Reeder vertraut jedoch seinen Kanälen zur italienischen Politik und den Zusagen, die er durch sie erhält: Meran werde eine jener wenigen Lizenzen bekommen, die trotz des allgemeinen Verbots in einigen italienischen Städten ein Casino erlaubt. Bennati glaubt an das Glücksspiel als Magnet für die Schönen und Reichen dieser Welt. Nur dank Poker und Roulette würde sich Meran in ein neues St. Moritz verwandeln und das hohe Preisniveau im Bristol halten lassen. 1952 spendiert er schon mal die Einrichtung für ein Spielzimmer im Kurhaus. Die „Bennati-Bar" wird mit venezianischen Spielkartenfiguren aus buntem Glas dekoriert. Auch im Bristol selbst lässt er Räume für ein künftiges Casino vorsehen. In den „roten Salon" im sechsten Stock führt ein eigener Lift.

Doch der Venezianer hat seine Kontakte zu den Behörden überschätzt. Er findet zwar den Anschluss an eine einflussreiche Seilschaft, der unter anderem der schillernde Präsident des Agip-Konzerns, Enrico Mattei, angehört. Bevor dieser 1962 unter mysteriösen Umständen beim Absturz seines Flugzeugs ums Leben kommt, ist er eine zentrale Figur im Nachkriegs-Italien. Dank Mattei wird Meran mehrmals zum Ziel der Autorallye „Supercortemaggiore" und zum Austragungsort eines Rundstreckenrennens für Sportwagen ausgewählt, das der legendäre Juan Manuel Fangio gewinnt. Die Genehmigung für ein Spielcasino aber will nicht eintreffen. Damit beginnen, kaum ist die erste Euphorie um das Bristol abgeklungen, auch schon Bennatis Probleme. Sie sind symptomatisch für ein Südtirol, in dem vieles in deutsche und italienische Einflusssphären getrennt und der Tourismus weitgehend eine Domäne der Deutschsprachigen ist. In den 1950er Jahren sieht es zwar noch einmal so aus, als könnten sich die Gewichte allmählich verlagern. So wird 1958 mit sehr viel Geld des Staates eine AG gegründet, die eine große Thermenanlage um die 25 Jahre zuvor entdeckten Radon-Quellen bauen soll. Die Thermen, der Pferderennplatz, das Bristol – dieses Dreigestirn hatte das Potenzial, Italienern die Tür zur Tourismusbranche zu öffnen. Doch mit den Thermen geht alles schief. Die Pläne für das neue Bad sind noch nicht fertig, als plötzlich das auffallend hohe Gesellschaftskapital von über einer Milliarde Lire verschwunden ist, verpulvert für ein dubioses Mineralwasserprojekt. So geht das neue Bad erst Anfang der 70er Jahre in einer sehr viel kleineren Ausführung in Betrieb und spielt nie die ihm zugedachte Rolle. Zugleich spürt Arnaldo Bennati, wie der Wind sich dreht. Drei Jahre nach der Eröffnung des Bristol proklamiert die Südtiroler Volkspartei ihr „Los von Trient", mit dem sie einen härteren Kurs einschlägt. Südtirol den Südtirolern, lautet nun die selbstbewusste Devise. Im Einzelnen lässt sich zwar nicht belegen, dass Bennati absichtlich Steine in den Weg gelegt werden. Aber für die Hubschrauberflüge nach Martell gibt es nie eine Genehmigung, die neue Straße ins hinterste Martelltal wird nicht gebaut, womit die Zufahrt zum Paradiso prekär bleibt – und das Bristol bleibt wie der Pferderennplatz ein feindliches Gebilde, für das man keinen Finger rührt. Selbst vom Staat ist nicht viel an Hilfe zu erwarten, wie Bennati an der verweigerten Lizenz für das Spielcasino sieht.

So vergeht dem Reeder allmählich der Spaß; auch weil das Bristol alles andere als ein gutes Geschäft ist. In seinen besten Tagen spielt es allenfalls die Betriebskosten ein, an eine Amortisierung des Kapitals ist nie zu denken. Die luxuriöse Ausstattung verlangte nach Zimmerpreisen, die in St. Moritz, New York oder Venedig zu bekommen sind, nicht aber in einem Provinznest wie Meran, das von besseren Zeiten träumt. Als Mitte der 1960er Jahre auch noch sein Sohn stirbt, zieht Bennati sich allmählich nach Venedig zurück. War ihm beim Bau des Bristol nichts zu teuer gewesen, dreht er plötzlich jede Lira fürs Hotel zweimal um. 1967 wird das Bristol von der Luxusklasse herabgestuft. Das Hotel kooperiert nun mit großen Reiseveranstaltern und senkt die Preise, was wiederum die Flicks und die Pirellis vertreibt. Eine Spirale, auf der es rasch nach unten geht.

Derweil rauscht der Fortschritt an dem Prachtbau vorbei. 1969 ist die Brennerautobahn zwischen Kufstein und Brenner durchgehend befahrbar, am Abschnitt bis Bozen wird gebaut. Der einsetzende Massentourismus kommt im Pkw daher und sucht das ländliche Idyll. In den einst armseligen Dörfern außerhalb Merans schießen Hotels im Tirolerstil aus dem Boden wie Pilze nach einem warmen Sommerregen. Meran erstickt derweil im Verkehr. Die einst vorzügliche Lage des Bristol zwischen den Promenaden und dem Bahnhof verkommt zur Randzone. Etliche der Großhotels aus der Jahrhundertwende müssen sich in eine neue Rolle als Schule oder Bürogebäude fügen. Auch dem Bristol kann all sein Luxus nicht helfen. Der neue Südtirol-Urlauber sucht urige Gemütlichkeit in Bauernstuben und nicht venezianischen Schnickschnack. 1979 zieht Bennati einen Schlussstrich. Das Paradiso in Martell verkauft er an die Brauerei Forst, die es seitdem verfallen lässt. An die hochtrabenden Pläne Bennatis erinnert nur das venezianische Rot, das von der Fassade blättert.

Das Bristol dagegen wird von einer Finanzgruppe übernommen, die den bekanntesten Hotelier in der Stadt zum Aushängeschild hat: Artur Eisenkeil ist Präsident des einflussreichen Südtiroler Hotelier- und Gastwirteverbandes und besitzt mit dem Meranerhof und dem Grandhotel Palace zwei der besten Häuser in Meran. Das deutschsprachige Südtirol ist erleichtert, scheint das „walsche" Bristol doch endlich in „richtige" Hände gekommen zu sein. Eisenkeil nimmt im Untergeschoss die Kurabteilung in Betrieb, die bereits 1954 vorgesehen, unter Bennati aber nie eröffnet worden war. Er lässt einige der Zimmer und Suiten sowie den großen Salon im sechsten Stock renovieren, und 1981 steigt im Bristol die Eröffnungsfeier der Schach-Weltmeisterschaft. Es ist nicht mehr als ein wehmütiger Nachklang der glamourösen Feste der Fünfzigerjahre. Eisenkeils Engagement kann das Sterben des Bristol nur verzögern, nicht aber verhindern.

Als er merkt, dass sein Partner Pietro Tosolini, der bekannteste Bauunternehmer Südtirols, nicht am Hotelbetrieb interessiert ist, sondern an der Kubatur und an den mit ihr verbundenen Baumöglichkeiten, steigt Eisenkeil 1984 aus. Tosolini lässt den Betrieb zunächst auf Sparflamme weiterlaufen. Bald ist aber auch der letzte Glanz des Bristol verblichen. 1991 erlebt es seine letzte Saison. In einem der folgenden kalten Winter zerbersten Rohre, das Wasser plätschert von den Balkonen, Perserteppiche vermodern. Eines Nachts ist ein großes Fenster im Parterre eingeschlagen. Was Tosolini bis dahin nicht hat sicherstellen lassen, verschwindet in der Dunkelheit: handbemalte Nachtkästchen, Lampen aus Muranoglas und aus der Rezeption Fotos und Zeitungsartikel, die vom Spleen eines reichen Reeders berichten. Fünfzehn Jahre steht das Bristol dann noch leer vor sich hin: der weiße Marmor schmutziggrau, die Rollläden schief im Wind, die Fenster wie erblindete Augen. 2006 endlich rücken Bagger und Presslufthämmer an, den letzten Rest eines Traumes zu zerstückeln – und Platz zu schaffen für ein geschichtsloses Wohn- und Geschäftszentrum mit Supermarkt und Einkaufspassagen.

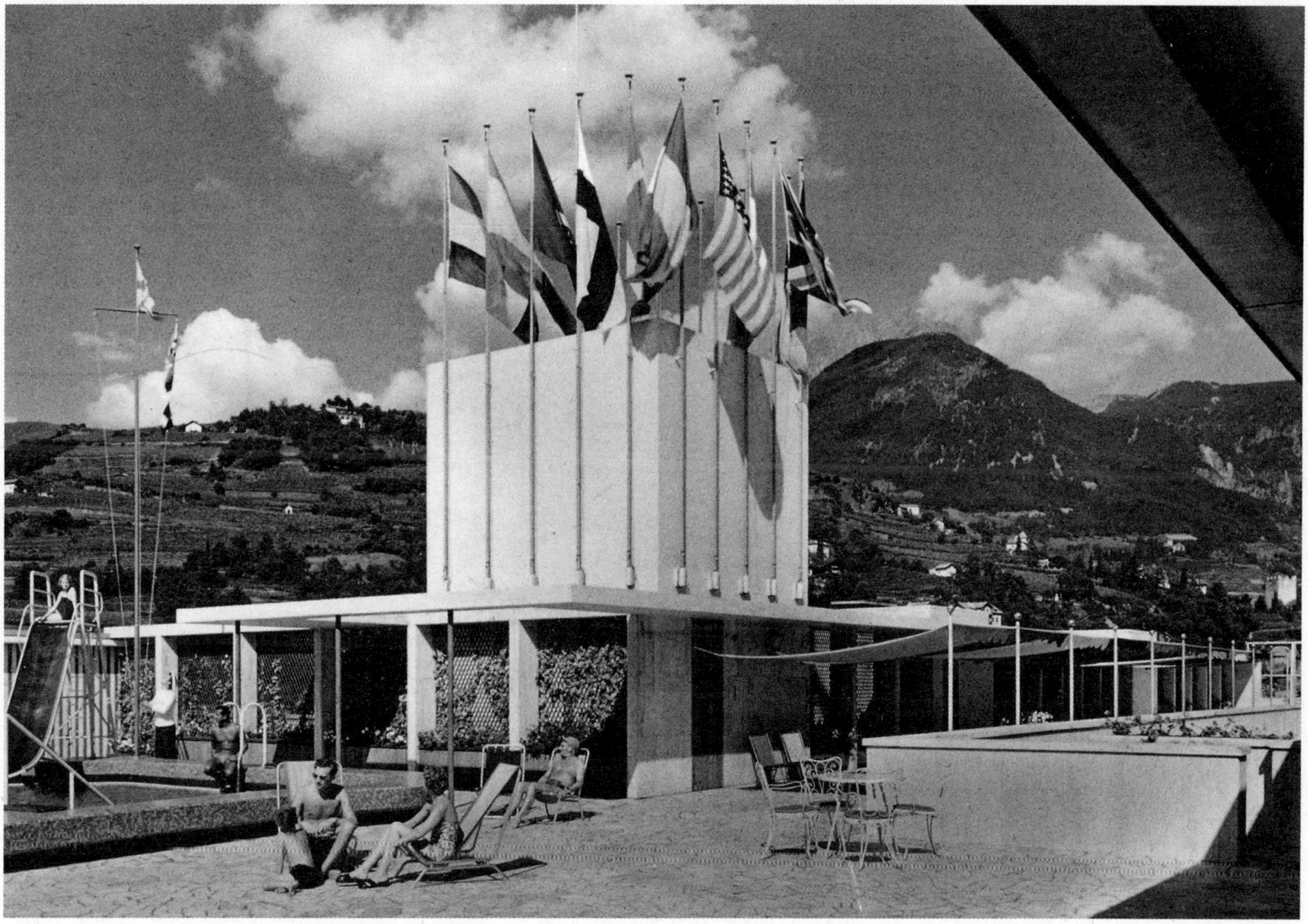

Hotel Bristol, la storia | Josef Rohrer

I tappeti nel grande salone sono avvolti ormai da tempo, i quadri sono scomparsi dalle pareti rivestite di seta, le lampade di vetro soffiato di Murano sono state smontate. Le ruspe e i martelli pneumatici avanzano e distruggono l'enorme edificio: il salone in cui ballava la giovane Sophia Loren, la facciata di marmo bianco, le eleganti scale, la piscina sul tetto tanto ammirata dalla stampa internazionale. Alla fine il Bristol di Merano è ridotto a un gigantesco cumulo di macerie e lamiere. È quel che resta del sogno di un ricchissimo armatore di Venezia che con il Bristol, inaugurato nel 1954 e considerato da numerosi giornali "l'hotel più moderno ed elegante d'Europa", voleva fare di Merano una seconda St. Moritz. In questo sogno egli investì enormi somme di denaro, ma la sorte gli fu avversa. Questo racconto narra in primo luogo dello splendore e del declino di uno straordinario hotel che venne costruito nel posto sbagliato, ma anche di molte altre interessanti vicende che si incrociano in esso e si intrecciano in un pezzo di storia contemporanea.

Le vicende del Bristol rispecchiano il tramonto della monarchia asburgica, la mania di grandezza del fascismo, il famigerato patto del 1939 tra Hitler e Mussolini, il breve accendersi in Alto Adige dell'orgoglio nazionale italiano dopo la seconda guerra mondiale e l'avvento del turismo di massa che ha mutato radicalmente il volto delle Alpi. Star più o meno famose, giocatori e speculatori, l'aristocrazia del denaro europea e un futuro papa: tutti passano dal Bristol. L'hotel è come un grande palcoscenico sul quale scorrono 100 anni di storia del Sudtirolo.

La storia del Bristol comincia agli inizi del '900, quando viene costruito il primo albergo con questo nome. Nella cosiddetta belle époque il Tirolo meridionale vive un breve periodo di splendore. La regione agricola un tempo arretrata prende il sopravvento sulla Boemia, che fino ad allora ha avuto un ruolo di primo piano, e diventa il luogo di villeggiatura più frequentato dell'impero austroungarico. È il boom del "balcone meridionale della monarchia", Merano è affollata. L'alta nobiltà e i nuovi ricchi provenienti dalla Germania, dalla Russia e dai paesi della corona asburgica vanno a spasso sulle *Promenaden*. Sorgono numerosi hotel. Il potenziale sembra illimitato e attira sempre più investitori. E così una famiglia di industriali tedesca costruisce nell'odierno Corso della Libertà un altro grand hotel nello stile dell'epoca. Il primo Bristol mostra orgoglioso la sua architettura neoclassica con frontoni e colonne, abbondanti stucchi e salotti riccamente arredati. Sei anni dopo scoppia la prima guerra mondiale. Come quasi tutti gli altri grandi alberghi di Merano, anche il Bristol si trasforma improvvisamente in un lazzaretto.

Dopo la fine della guerra il Sudtirolo viene separato dall'Austria; il "balcone meridionale della monarchia" diventa la provincia più settentrionale d'Italia. Gli italiani, che tra la fine dell'Ottocento e l'inizio del Novecento non avevano avuto alcun ruolo per l'economia turistica del Tirolo, ora prendono possesso della loro nuova provincia anche andandovi in villeggiatura. Con i primi turisti, nel 1921 giunge una drammatica notizia per il Bristol. L'Italia ha confiscato gli immobili dei cittadini tedeschi sul suo territorio come risarcimento per i danni di guerra. Senza questo esproprio la storia del Bristol sarebbe stata simile a quella di molti altri alberghi. Invece ha avuto degli sviluppi singolari. Il Bristol, come la maggior parte dei beni espropriati, viene ceduto all'Opera Nazionale per i Combattenti (ONC), un fondo per l'assistenza agli ex soldati italiani istituito dopo la disfatta di Caporetto per sollevare il morale delle truppe al fronte. In un primo momento l'ONC vuole vendere l'hotel. Poiché non si trovano acquirenti, l'apparato statale ora sotto il controllo di Mussolini decide di utilizzarlo per la sua politica di italianizzazione. Il Bristol è la pietra di un mosaico in cui l'economia del turismo altoatesino, dominato soprattutto dalla popolazione di lingua tedesca, assume i colori della bandiera italiana. Intorno al 1930 il famoso architetto milanese Paolo Vietti-Violi progetta per la città di Merano un enorme ippodromo. Mussolini si interessa personalmente a questo progetto e nel 1936 l'ippodromo viene inaugurato con il Gran Premio di Merano che da allora è una delle manifestazioni più importanti dell'ippica italiana. Quando nel 1932, non lontano dalla città, viene scoperta una sorgente di acque lievemente radioattive, Vietti-Violi progetta anche un centro termale che, se fosse stato realizzato, sarebbe diventato il più grande d'Europa. Intanto, un altro architetto milanese ha in mente qualcosa di grandioso. Gio Ponti, che in seguito diventerà famoso per il grattacielo Pirelli di Milano, progetta un gigantesco impianto sciistico sopra le Dolomiti tra Bolzano, la val Gardena e Cortina: 150 chilometri di impianti a fune con lussuose stazioni intermedie comprensive di hotel, centri commerciali e parchi divertimento. Ma anche questa grande idea rimane sulla carta. Degli alberghi progettati Ponti ne costruisce solamente uno, il Paradiso del Cevedale nel gruppo dell'Ortles, molto apprezzato per la sua architettura. La sua storia si incrocerà più tardi con quella del nuovo Hotel Bristol.

Al vecchio Bristol la gestione dell'ONC non giova. Nella metà degli anni Trenta gli hotel sorti a cavallo tra i due secoli hanno completamente perso il loro splendore. Quando poi bisogna anche applicare l'accordo sulle opzioni sottoscritto da Hitler e Mussolini, l'ONC per ragioni di stato deve mettere il Bristol a disposizione della "Amtliche Deutsche Ein- und Rückwanderungs-Stelle" (l'ufficio germanico per l'emigrazione e il rimpatrio), che ha il compito di organizzare il trasferimento volontario, deliberato da Hitler e Mussolini, dei cittadini sudtirolesi di lingua tedesca e ladina in una regione dell'Impero Tedesco.

Con l'entrata della Wehrmacht in Italia l'accordo sulle opzioni diventa cartastraccia e nel Bristol si trasferiscono gli uffici dell'esercito tedesco. Quando la guerra è finalmente finita, l'edificio non è più utilizzabile come hotel.

Ma come la fenice rinasce dalle sue ceneri, un nuovo Bristol sorge dalle macerie di quello vecchio. Alla fine degli anni Quaranta l'armatore veneziano Arnaldo Bennati arriva per caso a Merano. Accompagna nella città di cura uno dei suoi figli malato di cuore, che soffre di una grave forma di asma, e rimane affascinato da essa. Bennati, originario di Genova, dopo la guerra è uno degli uomini più ricchi dell'Italia del Nord. Possiede, oltre a una fiorente compagnia marittima, anche uno dei migliori hotel di Venezia, il Bauer-Grünwald. A Merano Bennati è allettato dalle opportunità che qui sembrano offrirglisi. Nel 1950 acquista il Bristol, in un periodo in cui il turismo è stagnante e parecchi grand hotel hanno chiuso i battenti. L'ONC è contentissima di essersi finalmente disfatta di questo immobile. Bennati in un primo momento ha intenzione di risanare l'edificio e di ampliarlo aggiungendovi un'ala. Poi però non esita a far demolire il vecchio Bristol; la tutela delle Belle Arti non esiste ancora. Al suo posto deve sorgere un nuovo Bristol più grande, un albergo che deve stupire tutto il mondo.

E il mondo si stupisce. Il nuovo hotel viene progettato dall'architetto veneziano Marino Meo, il quale inizialmente lo concepisce come un cubo con un cortile interno. Sono già stati costruiti due piani dell'edificio, quando Bennati ne fa demolire una parte. Il progetto, che prevedeva la piscina nel giardino davanti all'hotel, non gli pare abbastanza spettacolare. Soltanto il secondo progetto lo soddisfa. L'edificio di sei piani è a forma di H e la piscina profonda tre metri si trova – cosa mai vista prima – sul tetto. Per i lavori di costruzione, durati più di due anni, vengono spesi un miliardo e mezzo di lire. Con questa somma all'epoca si sarebbero potuti acquistare due degli alberghi più grandi di Firenze. Il Bristol è completamente climatizzato, un lusso che a quel tempo non si poteva permettere nemmeno il Waldorf-Astoria di New York. Tutte le 137 stanze e le 20 suite di lusso dispongono di una presa per l'antenna TV, anche se la televisione arriverà in regione soltanto due anni dopo. Dalla Persia Bennati fa arrivare un carico di tappeti, pare più di 1000, alti sei centimetri da stendere nello spettacolare salone dalle pareti di onice. Dal soffitto pende un lampadario con 1000 lampadine e 1500 placchette di vetro soffiato di Murano. Per realizzare le sue idee stravaganti l'armatore non bada a spese.

Ospite famosa della festa d'inaugurazione nell'estate del 1954 è la ventenne Sophia Loren, la nuova stella nel firmamento del cinema. Per la benedizione dell'hotel Bennati si rivolge al patriarca di Venezia, Angelo Giuseppe Roncalli, che poco dopo diventerà celebre come papa Giovanni XXIII. Mentre la maggior parte dei sudtirolesi vede il nuovo hotel come un "casermone" che rimarrà loro sempre estraneo, la stampa italiana e internazionale esalta il Bristol come uno dei "più moderni ed eleganti hotel d'Europa". Perfino il *New York Times* dedica un articolo al "modernissimo Bristol". Nei primi mesi della sua attività appaiono sui giornali 360 articoli sul nuovo albergo: la sua architettura e gli interni vengono considerati sensazionali. Nelle camere più costose maschere veneziane fungono da punto luce, le lampade in vetro di Murano sono cosparse di polvere d'oro, ovunque sono stati utilizzati marmi e legni pregiati, molte pareti sono rivestite di seta. E al bordo della piscina sul tetto, poi, si ha la sensazione di essere su una nave da crociera ancorata tra le montagne.

Tanto glamour è come una calamita per l'alta società. Dalle regioni italiane arrivano al Bristol i Pirelli e gli Invernizzi, magnati dell'industria alimentare, mentre dalla Germania giungono i Flick. Merano sembra ritornare ai bei tempi, quando – tra la fine dell'Ottocento e l'inizio del Novecento – l'alta nobiltà e l'aristocrazia del denaro europee vi si recavano per un soggiorno di cura. Al Bristol si tengono ora i congressi annuali dell'Automobilclub Italiano, accompagnati dalle apparizioni di Sophia Loren. Mike Bongiorno, la nuova star della televisione italiana, vi conduce uno show; sulla terrazza sul tetto si può assistere a sfilate di moda e le serate di gala in occasione del Gran Premio di Merano si svolgono naturalmente al Bristol. L'hotel si trasforma anche più volte in set per riprese cinematografiche come ad esempio nel 1957 per il film "Mein Schatz ist aus Tirol" ("Il mio tesoro è del Tirolo") interpretato dalle gemelle Kessler e Joachim Fuchsberger. Alcuni meranesi fanno da comparse in questo film: è una delle poche occasioni in cui la popolazione locale può avere accesso all'hotel. I camerieri e i cuochi tirolesi, infatti, vengono ritenuti non adatti a questo ambiente. Il personale deve corrispondere al flair mondano e viene da fuori. Arnaldo Bennati, però, non si accontenta di un solo albergo lussuosissimo, vuole avere di più. Subito dopo l'apertura del Bristol acquista in val Martello il Paradiso del Cevedale costruito da Gio Ponti nel 1936. Senza rispettare questo straordinario esempio di architettura moderna, eleva l'edificio di un piano, aggiunge un'ala e sostituisce al delicato verde oliva della facciata un forte rosso veneziano. L'hotel Paradiso a 2000 metri sopra il livello del mare viene concepito come una stravagante dependance del Bristol di Merano e del Bauer-Grünwald di Venezia, raggiungibile attraverso una nuova strada oppure in elicottero direttamente dal tetto del Bristol. I fantastici progetti di Bennati prevedono anche una funivia per collegare il Bristol con la Muta, una delle montagne che sovrasta la conca meranese. La visione di Bennati ruota attorno al gioco d'azzardo, nel quale l'imprenditore vede un nuovo impulso per il turismo. A Merano vi erano stati già parecchi tentativi per aprire un casinò. Prima e dopo le due guerre mondiali al Kurhaus si giocava a poker al limite della legalità, finché nel 1947 il gioco d'azzardo viene ufficialmente proibito. Ma l'armatore veneziano confida nei suoi contatti con i politici italiani e nelle promesse ricevute: Merano potrà ottenere una delle poche licenze che, nonostante il divieto generale, consentiranno ad alcune città italiane di possedere un casinò. Bennati è convinto che il gioco d'azzardo sia come una calamita per i cittadini facoltosi. Soltanto grazie al poker e alla roulette Merano potrebbe trasformarsi in una St. Moritz e contribuire a mantenere alto il livello dei prezzi del Bristol. Nel 1952 Bennati fa arredare a spese sue una stanza da gioco nel Kurhaus. Il Bar Bennati viene decorato con figure di carte da gioco veneziane in vetro colorato. Anche all'interno del Bristol sono previste delle sale per il casinò. Alla sala rossa situata al sesto piano si accede con un apposito ascensore. Tuttavia Bennati ha sopravvalutato i suoi rapporti con le autorità. Ha contatti con personaggi influenti tra cui anche Enrico Mattei, lo sfuggente presidente dell'Agip. Prima di perdere la vita nel 1962 in circostanze misteriose precipitando con il suo aereo, questi è sicuramente una personalità di rilievo nell'Italia del dopoguerra. Grazie a Mattei Merano viene più volte scelta come traguardo del rally Supercortemaggiore e designata come sede di una gara di corsa automobilistica che viene vinta dal leggendario Manuel Fangio. L'autorizzazione per l'apertura del casinò però non arriva.

Così – la prima euforia per il Bristol si è appena smorzata – cominciano per Bennati i problemi. Essi sono sintomatici di una provincia in cui vi è separazione tra sfere di competenza tedesche e italiane e il settore turistico è dominato soprattutto dalla popolazione di lingua tedesca. Negli anni Cinquanta sembra ancora una volta che l'asse della bilancia si possa spostare. Così nel 1958 viene fondata con grossi finanziamenti dello stato una società per azioni che ha il compito di costruire un grande impianto termale sul luogo dove 25 anni prima era stata scoperta una sorgente di radon. Le terme, l'ippodromo, il Bristol: questa triade avrebbe dovuto aprire le porte del turismo italiano.

Purtroppo la costruzione delle terme non va per il verso giusto. La progettazione non è ancora terminata quando il capitale della società, equivalente a più di un miliardo di lire, è improvvisamente svanito. Così, soltanto all'inizio degli anni Settanta, le terme vengono realizzate sulla base di un nuovo progetto di dimensioni minori, ma non avranno mai il ruolo ad esse originariamente attribuito. Allo stesso tempo Bennati avverte che la situazione politica sta cambiando. Tre anni dopo l'apertura del Bristol la Südtiroler Volkspartei proclama il suo "Los von Trient", con cui inizia a seguire una linea più dura. Il Sudtirolo ai Sudtirolesi: questo è il suo motto. Non è possibile dimostrare fino in fondo che Bennati è stato intenzionalmente ostacolato, ma l'autorizzazione per i voli in elicottero in val Martello non viene concessa così come non viene costruita la nuova strada nella valle, per cui l'accesso all'hotel Paradiso rimane precario. Inoltre il Bristol, come l'ippodromo, viene visto come qualcosa di ostile per cui non si muove un dito. Perfino dallo stato non ci si può aspettare un grande aiuto, come Bennati deve constatare dopo il rifiuto della licenza per il casinò.

Così l'armatore veneziano a poco a poco perde il suo entusiasmo, anche perché il Bristol si rivela tutt'altro che un buon affare. Nelle giornate migliori l'incasso copre tutt'al più le spese di gestione; un ammortamento del capitale è impensabile. Il lussuoso arredamento richiede dei prezzi pari a quelli di St. Moritz, New York o Venezia, ma impensabili per un luogo di provincia come Merano in attesa di tempi migliori. Quando alla metà degli anni Sessanta gli muore il figlio, Bennati si ritira a poco a poco a Venezia. Se per la costruzione del Bristol non aveva badato a spese, ora improvvisamente comincia a soppesare ogni lira. Nel 1967 il Bristol viene declassato dalla categoria di lusso. Decide quindi di collaborare con grandi operatori turistici e di abbassare i prezzi, il che allontana i Flick e i Pirelli. È una spirale che porta rapidamente verso il basso. Intanto fuori dallo sfarzoso edificio avanza il progresso. Nel 1969 l'autostrada del Brennero da Kufstein al Brennero è interamente transitabile, mentre il tratto fino a Bolzano è in costruzione. Sono gli inizi del turismo di massa: i nuovi ospiti arrivano in macchina e cercano una natura idilliaca. Nei dintorni di Merano gli hotel in stile tirolese spuntano come funghi dopo una calda pioggia estiva. Intanto la città è soffocata dal traffico. La posizione del Bristol tra le passeggiate e la stazione da centrale diventa periferica. Parecchi grand hotel costruiti tra la fine dell'Ottocento e l'inizio del Novecento devono adattarsi al nuovo ruolo di scuole o uffici. Nemmeno il Bristol, con tutto il suo lusso, può sottrarsi al suo declino. I turisti che giungono in Alto Adige cercano l'atmosfera accogliente nelle tipiche *Stuben* tirolesi e non tra le cianfrusaglie veneziane. Nel 1979 Bennati decide di rinunciare ai suoi alberghi nella provincia di Bolzano. Il Paradiso in val Martello viene venduto alla birreria Forst, che lo lascia andare in rovina. Soltanto il rosso veneziano che si sfalda sulla facciata ricorda i grandiosi progetti di Bennati.

Il Bristol, invece, viene rilevato da una società finanziaria cui appartiene il più noto albergatore di Merano, Artur Eisenkeil, presidente dell'influente unione albergatori e pubblici esercenti sudtirolesi, che possiede con il Meranerhof e il Grand Hotel Palace due degli alberghi più belli di Merano. Il Sudtirolo di lingua tedesca si sente sollevato, il *walsches* Bristol sembra finalmente finito nelle mani "giuste". Eisenkeil mette in funzione il reparto cure nel seminterrato, già previsto nel 1954, ma mai aperto. Fa rinnovare alcune stanze e suite, nonché la grande sala al sesto piano; nel 1981 al Bristol si svolge la festa d'inaugurazione del campionato mondiale di scacchi. Ma non è che una malinconica eco delle splendide feste degli anni Cinquanta. L'impegno di Eisenkeil può soltanto rinviare, ma non impedire la fine del Bristol.

Quando si accorge che il suo socio Pietro Tosolini, il più noto imprenditore edile dell'Alto Adige, non è interessato all'hotel, bensì alla cubatura dell'edificio e alle prospettive edilizie ad essa collegate, nel 1984 Eisenkeil si ritira. Tosolini inizialmente lascia in funzione l'albergo all'insegna del risparmio. Ma presto sbiadisce anche l'ultimo splendore del Bristol che vive la sua ultima stagione nel 1991. Durante un inverno freddo scoppiano dei tubi, l'acqua scorre giù dai balconi, i tappeti persiani marciscono. Una notte viene rotta una grande finestra al pianterreno. Ciò che Tosolini non ha ancora fatto mettere al sicuro, sparisce: comodini dipinti a mano, lampade di vetro di Murano e, dalla reception, fotografie e articoli di giornale che raccontano delle stramberie di un ricco armatore. Per quindici anni il Bristol rimane vuoto e mostra il marmo bianco divenuto grigio sporco, le tapparelle curve nel vento e le finestre come occhi accecati. Nel 2006 le ruspe e i martelli pneumatici riducono in pezzi quel che resta di un sogno, per far posto a un centro abitativo e commerciale senza storia.

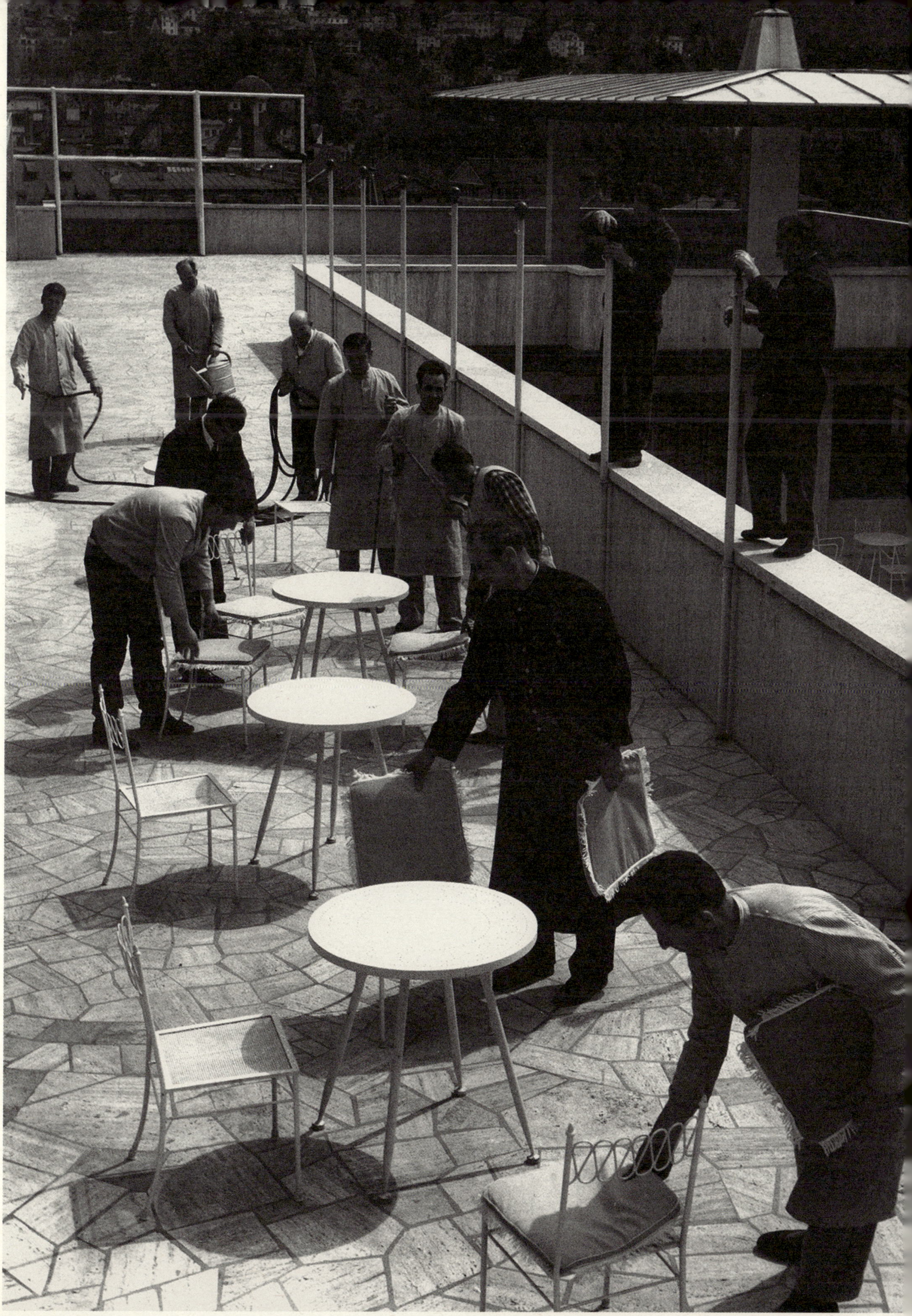

Hotel Bristol. The Story | Josef Rohrer

The carpets in the large salon have long been rolled up, the pictures have disappeared from the silk-covered walls, and the lamps made of mouth-blown Murano glass have been taken down. Excavators and pneumatic hammers have approached and are gnawing their way through the enormous building: through the hall in which young Sophia Loren had danced, through the white marble facade, through the elegant staircase, up to the roof terrace with the swimming pool that was so admired by the international press. In the end, the Bristol in Merano lies there, crushed to a huge pile of debris and steel. The residues of an affluent Venetian shipping-company owner's dream. By means of the Bristol, opened in 1954 and lauded in countless newspaper articles as the "most modern and elegant hotel in Europe", he wanted to turn Merano into a second St. Moritz. He invested enormous sums in this dream – and failed.

On the surface, this story is about the glory and ruin of an unusual hotel that was built in the wrong place. Underneath the surface, however, several exciting stories intertwine and are woven to a passage in contemporary history. The Bristol reflects the decline of the decadent Habsburg Monarchy, the megalomania of Mussolini's fascism, the infamous treaty of 1939 between Hitler and Mussolini, the brief sparks of Italian national pride in South Tyrol after World War II, and the invasion of mass tourists who radically changed the face of the Alps. Stars and starlets, gamblers and speculators, Europe's moneyed aristocracy, and a future pope – they all appeared at the Bristol. The hotel is a stage on which one hundred years of South Tyrolean history were performed in quick-motion. The story of the Bristol began shortly after 1900, with a previous building by the same name. During the alleged Belle Époque, the southern part of Tyrol had its brief heyday. What was once a backward farming region overtook Bohemia, which had been the leading province until then, and became the most popular holiday region in Austria-Hungary. The "southern balcony of the monarchy" boomed, and Merano brimmed over with visitors. The higher nobility as well as the *nouveaux riches* from Germany, Russia, and the Austrian crown estates strolled along the promenades, and many new hotels were built. The potential seemed to be unlimited and attracted ever new investors. So it came that, next to today's Statue of Liberty, a German industrial family built another large hotel in the style of the times. The first Bristol proudly presented its neoclassical outfit with its gables and pillars, its overflow of stucco, and its opulent business rooms. Six years later, World War I started. Like almost all the other rather large hotels in Merano, the Bristol was converted to a military hospital overnight.

After the war, South Tyrol was separated from Austria, and the southern balcony of the monarchy became the most northern province of Italy. Italians, who had not been among the tourists in Tyrol around the turn of the century, started to travel around and explore their new province. Along with the first tourists in 1921, the Bristol received a dramatic message. Italy had confiscated the real-estate of German citizens in its territory as a compensation for war damage. Without this expropriation, the story of the Bristol would have resembled that of many other hotels. But now it was taking a new turn. Like most of the expropriated buildings and properties, the Bristol was transferred to the "Opera Nazionale per i Combattenti" (ONC), a relief fund for former Italian front-line veterans that had been founded after the lost "Battle of Karfreit" to boost the morale of the soldiers. At first, the ONC wanted to sell the hotel, but no buyer was found, so the state machinery – now under Mussolini – decided to use it for its Italianisation policy.

The Bristol became a little stone in a mosaic that was meant to add the *Tricolore* shades to the tourism industry in South Tyrol which was then largely dominated by speakers of German. Around 1930, the star architect Paolo Vietti-Violi from Milan planned a huge horse race track in Merano. Mussolini himself dealt with the project. In 1936, it was inaugurated with the "Gran Premio di Merano". Flat racing has been one of the highlights in Italian equestrian sports ever since. When, in 1932, springs with slightly radioactive water were discovered near Merano, Vietti-Violi also a planned thermal spring facility, which would have become the largest in Europe at that time. But it was never built. Another Milan architect also had big plans: Gio Ponti, who later became famous with the Pirelli skyscraper in Milan, designed a huge ski-lift network that was meant to join Bolzano, Gröden and Cortina and span across the entire Dolomites range. A 150 kilometres long funicular railway, interrupted by luxurious halfway stations that were designed as hotel facilities, shopping centres, and entertainment parks, all in one. Yet, this sweeping venture also remained a sketch on paper. Of all the hotel facilities he had planned, Ponti only realised the prototype "Paradiso del Cevedale" in the Ortler Group which was much praised for its architecture. Its history later coincided with that of the new Bristol.

The ONC management was unfavourable to the old Bristol. By the mid-thirties, the glory of the turn-of-the-century hotel had faded for the most part. And when the Option Agreement between Hitler and Mussolini had to be implemented, reasons of state forced the ONC to make space for the "*Amtliche Deutsche Ein- und Rückwanderungs-Stelle*" [Official German Immigration and Remigration Office] in the Bristol. As of 1939, this office was meant to organise the resettlement of the German and Ladin-speaking South Tyroleans to a new territory in the German Reich, as resolved by Hitler and Mussolini. But when the German Armed Forces marched into Italy, the so-called Option Agreement was no longer at issue. Now, German army officials moved into the Bristol. When the war was finally over, it could hardly be used as a hotel any more.

Like a phoenix from the ashes, however, a new Bristol grew out of the old one. In the late forties, the Venetian shipping-company owner Arnaldo Bennati happened to visit Merano. One of his sons suffered from a heart disease and heavy asthma, so he accompanied him to a cure and fell in love with the city. A Genoan by birth, Bennati was one of the richest men in Northern Italy after the war. In addition to his flourishing shipping company, he also owned the Bauer-Grünwald Hotel, which was one of the best in Venice. Bennati was pleased by the many possibilities that seemed to present themselves to him in Merano. In 1950, he bought the Bristol, at a time when tourism was stagnating and many of the large Merano hotels remained closed. The ONC was glad to have gotten rid of the building at last. Bennati first considered renovating it and adding a side wing. But then he unceremoniously had it torn down; there were no such things as official preservation orders in those days. He wanted a new, larger Bristol instead, one the whole world would marvel about.

And marvel it did. The new Bristol was planned by the Venetian ship architect Marino Meo. The first design was a cube with a patio. When it was already two floors high, Bennati had parts of it demolished again. The concept with a swimming pool in the front garden was not spectacular enough for him. Only the second draft made him happy. The building was now shaped like an H, and the three metres deep swimming pool was on the roof terrace on the sixth floor. The world had not seen anything like it. When the new Bristol was finished after more than two years of construction, it had cost the incredible amount of 1.5 billion lire. In those days, one could have purchased two of the largest hotels in Florence for that money. The Bristol was fully air-conditioned – a luxury not even the Waldorf-Astoria in New York afforded itself then. All 137 rooms and twenty luxury suites had a television socket, although television was only introduced in the region two years later. And Bennati had a whole shipload of carpets come from Persia, allegedly more than 1000. In the spectacular salon with its walls of onyx, they were laid six centimetres high. In the chandelier above, 1500 thin mouth-blown Murano glass plates held 1000 light bulbs. Nothing was too expensive for the shipping-company owner's reverie.

The special guest at the opening celebration in summer 1954 was twenty-year old Sophia Loren, the new shooting star in the movie business. And the blessing for the new Bristol was given by the Patriarch of Venice, Angelo Giuseppe Roncalli, who became famous as Pope John XXIII not long afterwards. For most South Tyroleans, the new hotel was simply an "Italian box" that remained a foreign object to them, but the Italian and international press published countless articles in which the Bristol was praised as one of the "most modern and elegant hotels in Europe". Even the New York Times brought out a large article on the "conspicuously modern Bristol". In the first months, 360 articles were published on the new hotel; its architecture and interior were considered a sensation. In the better rooms, there were Venetian carnival figures as lamps, gold dust was sprinkled into the wall sconces made of Murano glass, there was marble and precious wood everywhere, and many of the walls were covered with silk wallpaper. And no later than when one had reached the pool on the roof, it felt as if one were on board a luxury liner that had dropped anchor in the mountains.

So much glamour attracted the high society. Italy's upper classes now resided at the Bristol. The Pirellis came, so did the food industrialists Invernizzi, as well as the Flicks from Germany. Merano seemed to be picking up the threads of its prime at the turn of the century, when the European high nobility and moneyed aristocracy came for a cure. The Italian Automobile Association now held its annual meetings at the Bristol, accompanied by Sophia Loren's appearances. Mike Bongiorno, the star of young Italian television, presented a show there, fashion shows were held on the roof terrace, and the gala evenings for the Gran Prize of Merano now took place at the Bristol, of course. Again and again, the hotel was also used as a film setting, like in 1957 for *Mein Schatz ist aus Tirol* [My Sweetheart is from Tyrol] with the Kessler twins and Joachim Fuchsberger. In this sentimental German film with a regional background, Merano citizens played bit parts which gave them the rare opportunity to see the Bristol from inside. After all, no Tyrolean waiters or chefs were employed there. The staff was to match the sophisticated flair, so it had to come from elsewhere.

But Arnaldo Bennati wanted more than just one unusual hotel. Not long after the opening of the Bristol, he purchased the "Paradiso del Cevedale" in the Martell Valley built by Gio Ponti in 1936. Regardless of this extraordinary example of modern hotel architecture, he had one floor and a wing added and painted a bright Venetian red over the soft olive green. He envisioned the "Paradiso", 2000 metres above sea level, as an extravagant branch of the Bristol in Merano and the Bauer-Grünwald in Venice, accessible not only via a new road, but also by a helicopter shuttle service that was to depart from the roof of the Bristol. Bennati's fantastic ideas were rounded off by a funicular railway that was supposed to run from the Bristol to the Muta – one of the mountains near Merano. And his brave new world of tourism should be based on gambling. Several attempts had been made to establish a casino in Merano. Before and after the two World Wars, people had gambled and played poker at the casino of the health resort, but only in dim light and semi-legally. In 1947, gambling was officially prohibited. Still, the shipping-company owner relied on his connections to Italian politicians and the promises they had made: he was told Merano would be granted one of the few licenses to open a casino, despite the general prohibition. Bennati was convinced that gambling would attract beautiful and rich people from all over the world. Only with poker and roulette, Merano would become a new St. Moritz, and it would be possible to maintain the high prices at the Bristol. In 1952, he already purchased the interior of a gambling room for the health resort. The "Bennati-Bar" was decorated with Venetian card figures made of stained glass. Even at the Bristol, he reserved rooms for a future casino. A separate lift led to the "Red Salon" on the sixth floor.

But the Venetian had overestimated his influence on the authorities. He did gain access to a powerful network that included the elusive president of the Agip company group, Enrico Mattei, who was a core figure in post-war Italy, before he died in 1962 in a mysterious plane crash. Thanks to Mattei, Merano was frequently chosen as the final destination of the motor rally "Supercortemaggiore" and became the venue of a road race for sports cars that was won by the legendary Juan Manuel Fangio. But no casino permission was granted. No sooner had the initial euphoria about the Bristol subsided than Bennati's problems began. They were symptomatic for a South Tyrol where German and Italian spheres of influence were strictly separated, and tourism was largely a domain of the German-speaking community. In the fifties, things once again looked as though the tables might gradually turn. In 1958, for instance, the government paid a large amount of money to found a limited company that should build the large thermal facility around the radon springs discovered twenty-five years earlier. The thermal springs, the horse race course, and the Bristol – this triumvirate had the potential to open the gates of the tourism industry for Italians. But everything went wrong with the springs. The plans for the new bathing house had not even been completed when suddenly the conspicuously high share capital of more than one billion lire disappeared, blown for a dubious mineral water project. So the new bathing complex was only opened on a much smaller scale in the early seventies and never played the important role it was supposed to. At the same time, Arnaldo Bennati felt the wind of change. Three years after the Bristol was opened, the South Tyrolean People's Party announced its "Break with Trient!" which was the beginning of a tougher policy. "South Tyrol for South Tyroleans" was the new confident motto. We do not know for sure whether obstacles were deliberately placed in Bennati's path. But he never received permission for the helicopter flights to Martell, the new road to the far end of Martell Valley was never built, so the access to the Paradiso remained precarious – and the Bristol as well as the horse race course continued to be enemy objects for which nobody would lift a finger. Even the government did not do much to help, as the refused casino license showed. Little by little, the shipping-company owner became fed up, especially because the Bristol was not good business, either. On its best days, it barely yielded the overhead costs, but an amortisation of the capital was way out of reach. The luxurious interior required room prices that were not even paid in St. Moritz, New York, or Venice, least of all in a backwater town like Merano that was only dreaming of better days. When his son died in the mid-sixties, Bennati gradually withdrew back to Venice. Money had not been an issue when he built the Bristol, but now he thought twice before spending another lira on it. In 1967, the Bristol was downgraded and no longer considered a luxury hotel. It now cooperated with tour operators and lowered its prices, which drove out the Flicks and Pirellis. From there, it was a fast downward spiral.

In the meanwhile, progress passed the stately building by. In 1969, the Brenner motorway was fit for traffic from Kufstein to the Brenner, and the section to Bolzano was under construction. The new mass tourists came by car and were longing for a countryside idyll. In the once wretched villages outside of Merano, all of a sudden Tyrolean-style hotels popped up like mushrooms after a warm summer rain, and Merano started to choke with traffic. The once first-rate location of the Bristol, between the promenades and the train station, became a marginal one. Many of the grand turn-of-the-century hotels were converted into schools or office buildings. All the luxury of the Bristol could not help it, either. The new holiday makers in South Tyrol came for cosiness in rustic rooms, not for Venetian twaddle. In 1979, Bennati rang down the curtain. He sold the Paradiso in Martell to the Forst brewery, which has been letting it go to ruin ever since. Only the Venetian red that is flaking off the facade is a reminder of Bennati's high-flying plans.

The Bristol was taken over by a group of financiers that included the city's best-known hotelier. Artur Eisenkeil was the president of the influential *Südtiroler Hotelier- und Gastwirteverband* [South Tyrolean Association of Hoteliers and Proprietors] and the owner of the Meranerhof as well as the Grandhotel Palace, two of the best hotels in Merano. German-speaking South Tyrol was relieved to hear that the "Italian box" was in the "right" hands, at last. Eisenkeil opened the health care facilities in the basement that had already been planned since 1954, but were never used under Bennati. He had some of the rooms and suites as well as the large salon on the sixth floor renovated, and in 1981, the opening ceremony for the World Chess Championship took place at the Bristol. Yet, it was but a wistful echo of the glamorous festivals of the fifties. Eisenkeil's commitment was only able to delay the death of the Bristol, not to prevent it. When he noticed that his partner, Pietro Tosolini, the best-known property developer in South Tyrol, was not interested in the hotel business, but only in the cubic content of the building and the construction possibilities bound up with it, Eisenkeil backed out in 1984. At first, Tosolini continued the business on the back burning, but soon the last bit of the Bristol's glory had faded. In 1991, it had its last season. During one of the following cold winters, pipes burst, water ran down the balcony, and the Persian carpets started to rot. One night, a large window on the ground floor was smashed. Whatever Tosolini had not secured by then, disappeared into the darkness: hand-painted bedside lockers, Murano glass lamps, and from the reception, photographs and newspaper articles that told of the reverie of a wealthy shipping-company owner. For another fifteen years, the Bristol still stood there, empty. Its white marble was filthy, its shutters hung crooked, its windows were as blunt as blind eyes. In 2006, the excavators and pneumatic hammers finally approached to shatter the last residues of a dream – and make space for a residential and business centre with a supermarket and shopping arcades, but without a story to tell.

131

Mit freundlicher Unterstützung von
con il gentile sostegno di
with the generous assistance of

AUTONOME PROVINZ BOZEN SÜDTIROL / PROVINCIA AUTONOMA DI BOLZANO ALTO ADIGE
Deutsche Kultur und Familie   Cultura tedesca e Famiglia

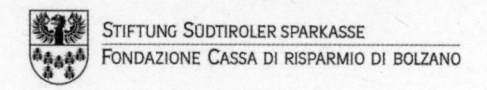

IMPRESA COSTRUZIONI - BAUUNTERNEHMUNG
HABITAT SPA-AG
via Roen Str. 53 - BOLZANO/BOZEN - Tel./Fax. 0471/270888

STIFTUNG SÜDTIROLER SPARKASSE
FONDAZIONE CASSA DI RISPARMIO DI BOLZANO

MARTIN GEIER GALERIE GALLERIA
39022 Algund (BZ) Italy
Josef-Weingartner-Straße 83
Tel. 0473 22 06 65

palbox®
pallets & containers

antonella cattani
contemporary art
via rosengarten str. 1/a
I - bolzano 39100 bozen
T.F. +39 0471 981884
info@accart.it - www.accart.it

artMbassy BERLIN
www.artmbassy.com

STIFTUNG SÜDTIROLER SPARKASSE
FONDAZIONE CASSA DI RISPARMIO DI BOLZANO
1854

**Wir stiften Kultur
Promuoviamo cultura**

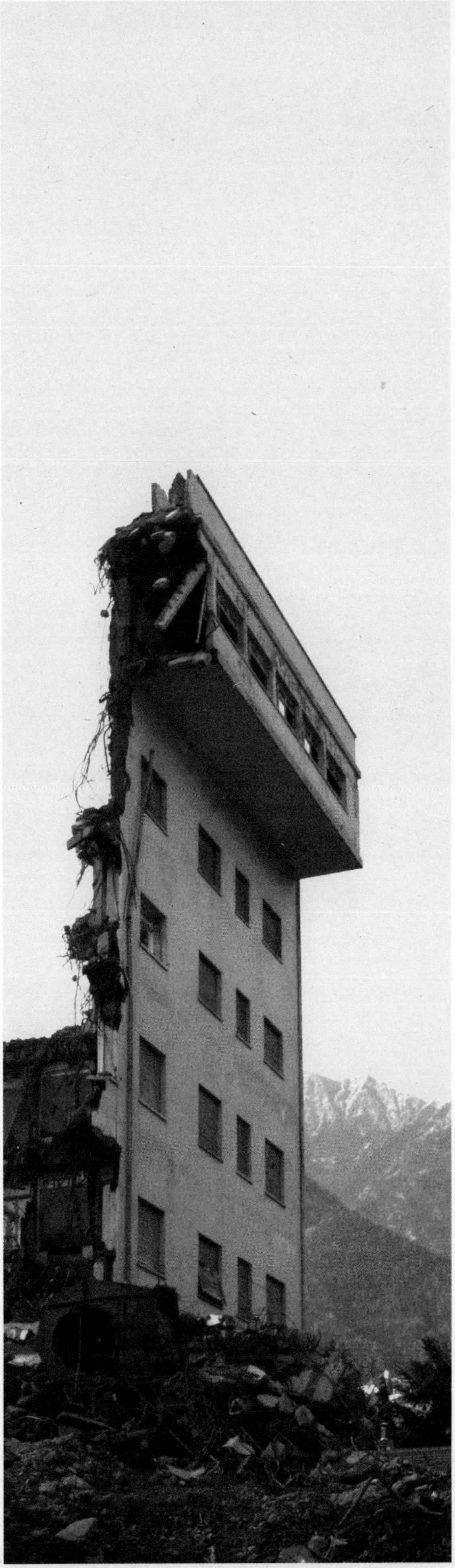